THE NEW CREATION

Copyright © David Gowon 2018
ISBN: 978-1-9164444-0-9

Published and Printed by:
Gracehouse Publishing
56, Gosport Road, Walthamstow,
London, United Kingdom, E17 7LY

Unless otherwise indicated, all Scripture quotations are taken from the King James Version (KJV) of the Bible.

All rights reserved.
No portion of this book may be used without the written permission of the publisher, with the exception of brief excerpts in magazines, articles, reviews, etc.

The Foreword

The New Creation is an all-time revelatory teaching that re-emphasise as well as challenge every Christian towards their identity in Christ. New creation realities teach that when you got born again, you became a new person and still. It teaches that your old sinful nature has passed away. It teaches that you are born of God. The nature of God is born in you. You are a new creature, brand new specie. Therefore, you must learn how to live your new life just as a newborn baby must learn to do certain things in this world. (I Peter 2:2)

Leadership experts will tell you that in an organizational structure, everything rises and falls on leadership. The same concept is with the subject of New Creation; the believer's life stems and ends with his/her identity in Christ. This is why the study of new creation reality is very crucial in that it is impossible to live out the victorious and blessed life offered to every believer by the freewill of Jesus Christ according to the Holy scriptures, "being justified freely by His grace through the redemption that is in Christ Jesus," (Romans 3:24). This is very important because the foundation of every Christian's accomplishment or fulfilment lies in the knowledge of their true identity in Christ.

In 1 Peter 2:9, Apostle Peter writes about the believer's identity and he says that "we are a chosen generation, a royal priesthood, a holy nation, God's own special people, that we may proclaim the praises of Him who called us out of darkness into His marvellous light". It is very important that as Christians we know why Peter points out the believer's identity in Christ as this will determine the outcome of our Christian walk. What this means is that as believers your new identity in Christ gives you not only the right but the capacity to publicly proclaim the praises of God because you are now a child of God (see John 1:12).

In my 15 years plus of being in Christian ministry, I have now come to the understanding that most battle in the pursuit of destiny is either lost on the ground of false identity or won through our new creation reality. In the book of Genesis Chapter three, the bible records the first account of 'Destiny Battle' lost to Satan because man was deceived to believe he was something else less likely to be God. The same is with many Christians today who allow Satan deceive them from believing and walking in the reality of there new nature in Christ. Satan is liar, there is not truth in him and therefore you must know that as a child of God are the exact opposite of whatever or whoever he says you are. You are who God says you are now that you are in Christ. Failure, sickness, diseases and poverty are no longer part of your nature.

Its so beneficial when a believer discovers and operates in/her identity in Christ because as a believer your identity precedes your authority, reveals your ability, defines your community and determine your prosperity. it's like all your capabilities are switched on once you come into the understanding and revelation of your nature in Christ. For every Christian seeking to understand his/her new nature in Christ; in this book is the perfect place to look. I have not only listen but sat down in discussions on a few occasions with Pastor David Gowon on the subject of new creation realities and I am still in awe of his in-depth understanding as well as his convictions of this life of grace. I have no doubt that every chapter will ignite a deeper desire in your heart and everyone who finds this book in their hands.

Thank you Pastor David, for pouring your heart and most importantly the unadulterated truth of God's word into this book, especially in a time like this where there is a rising generation of young believers seeking to understand what life in Christ really offers and what makes them different from the rest of the world. May the Lord continue to inspire more truth such as the one written in this book, so that many around the world can find liberation and illumination in Jesus name, Amen.

Apostle Femi Adun
President, Eagle World Outreach UK

NEW CREATION / 04

Who is God?

Who created the universe? God.

Describe God:

1. Always was and always has been.
2. Never can be created or destroyed.
3. All that ever was and always will be.
4. Always move into form through form and out of form.
5. God is the supreme being.
6. God is greater than everything in heaven and on earth.
7. He is the creator of the universe and in control of it.
8. He is without limitation.
9. He is all powerful, almighty (Gen 17:1).

10. He is the Alpha and Omega. The beginning and the ending (Rev 1:8).

11. He is the first and the last (Rev 1:11,17).

12. Nothing is too hard for him (Jer 23:17; Matt 19:26).

The compound names of God:

1. Omnipresent: He is everywhere present (Jer 23:23–24; Matt 28:20).

2. Omnipotent: This means all powerful, mighty (Gen 17:1). Nothing is too difficult for him (Jer 23:17).

3. Omniscient: Which means, he is all knowing and he knows all things. There is nothing hidden from him (Ps 139:1–4).

4. Self-existent: He is the beginning and was not created. Gen 1:1, "In the beginning was God. . . ", Ps 90:2, "Everlasting to everlasting you are God", Isa 44:6, "I am the first and I am the last and besides me there is no God", Rev 1:8, "I am Alpha and Omega, the beginning and the ending", Rev 1:17–18, "Fear not; I am the first and the last".

5. Self-sufficient: God is complete in himself and He

lacks nothing. John 1:3–5 "Through Him all things were made and without Him was not anything made that was made"; He is the maker of all things. Mal 3:6 "For I am the Lord God of Israel, I change not therefore ye sons of Jacob are not consumed." Heb 13:8 "Jesus Christ the same yesterday and today and forever".

Hebrew names of God:

1. ELOHIM means supreme God.
2. EL means mighty one.
3. EL-OLYON means the most high.
4. EL-SHADDAI means the mighty God.
5. ADONAI means Lord, Owner, Master, Ruler.
6. EL OLAM means the everlasting God.
7. JEHOVAH means I am (Exod 6:2–3).

Jehovah:

Jehovah reveals to us more about God's character and love (Exod 6:2–3):

1. Jehovah Jireh: The Lord will provide.
2. Jehovah Rapha: The Lord our healer.
3. Jehovah Nissi: The Lord our banner.
4. Jehovah Shalom: The Lord our peace.

5. Jehovah Raah: The Lord our Shepherd
6. Jehovah Tsidkenu: The Lord our righteousness.
7. Jehovah Sabaoth: The Lord of Host.
8. Jehovah Shammah: The Lord is present.

Contents

Foreword | 03

Who is God | 05

Chapter 1

The New Creation | 15

    Who is the New Creation? | 15

    Born of God | 16

    Salvation by Grace | 16

    The abundant Life | 17

    You are the blessed | 19

    The ability of God within us | 20

    Let God's Word abide in you | 21

    Who is man? | 22

You have the Holy Spirit in you	| 23
Recreation of the human spirit	| 24
The fruit of the created human spirit	| 29
The soul of man	| 29
The renewal of the mind	| 30
Sanctifying the thoughts	| 30
Renewed by the word of God	| 31
The body and its discipline	| 31
You are translated	| 32
Remission for the unsaved	| 35
Forgiveness for the Christian	| 35

Chapter 2

Who the Christian really is | 39

We are united with the Father and Son Jesus	| 39
You are a New Creation	| 45
Born into God's family	| 47
The New Creation is born of God	| 47
You are peculiar	| 49
You have dominion over the world	| 50

God's reasons for salvation	53
What is truth	54
What it means to be a Christian	55
I can do mentality	59
You are a winner	60
You are the righteousness of God	63
You have God's wisdom	64
You are complete in Him	65

Chapter 3

How to use the name of Jesus — | 67

Chapter 4

Your rights in Christ — | 73

You have Righteousness	73
You have Eternal Life	75
You have the right to choose	79
You have the right to live	80
You have the right to rule	82
You have an inheritance in Christ	82
You are God's address	83

"Ye are gods!"		88
God's mirror principle		94
Operation of the five senses		95

Chapter 5

The Person of the Holy Spirit | 97

Who is the Holy Spirit?		98
Every Christian can receive the Holy Spirit		105
Fellowship with the Spirit		106
His ministry through Christians		108

Chapter 6

The importance of the Holy Spirit in a Christian's life | 111

Speaking in tongues and its purposes		112
The gifts of the Holy Spirit		114
Ministry gifts		116
Difference between the gifts of the Holy Spirit and ministry gifts		119
Differences between the gifts of the Holy Spirit and fruit of the recreated human spirit		120

    Every Christian can walk in the power
    of the Holy Spirit | 120

Chapter 7

The Church of Christ | 125

    What is the universal Church and how
    do I become a member? | 125

    The purpose of the Church and its
    local assemblies | 126

    "Upon this rock I'll build my church" — is the
    rock Peter? | 128

    Is it important to belong to a church? | 129

    Who builds the church | 130

    Why should I go to Church? | 131

The Great Exchange | 133

Prayer Of Salvation | 137

Testimonials and Contacts | 139

NEW CREATION / 14

Chapter 1

THE NEW CREATION

9. Emmanuel: God with us.

Further scripture for study: Ps 138:2; John 1:14; 8:51–58; 1John 1:1,2; Col 1:26–27.

The New Creation seeks to examine by reason of divine revelation, the nature and life of the man in Christ and the effect of the regenerative power of Christ in his spirit, soul and body. The first chapter will basically examine the totality of the new creation, which is composed of three major sections:

1. The life of the regenerated human spirit.

2. The soul and the renewal of the mind.

3. The body and its discipline (subjection)

The New Creation is more than being baptised or confirmed. It is receiving the Life and Nature of God. Our spirits are recreated by receiving Eternal Life.

Who is the New Creation?

The new creation is the born again man, created in Christ Jesus. 2Corinthians 5:17 says "therefore if any man be in Christ, he is a new creature: Old things are passed away; behold all things are become new." This scripture shows that the new creation is not the "reformed". He never existed; he has a new life in the spirit, created in Christ Jesus.

Ephesians 2:10 says, "For we are his workmanship, created in Christ Jesus unto good works. . . " This goes further to show that the new creation life begins the moment he comes into Christ, because there are no traces of his past. For the new creation, being in Christ Jesus is the first right choice to life, as traditions of men, and other primordial considerations such as tribe, colour, wealth and age do not count (Galatians 6:15).

Born of God

The new creation is born of God. When God gave birth, He gave birth to us, because we believed in Him, we received his divine nature into our spirits. Wewere given birth to through His word. According to John 1:12–13, the natural man is born of blood, of the will of the flesh and of the will of man unto a perishable life. But the new creation is born of God. 1Peter 1:23 says, "being born again, not of corruptible seed, but of incorruptible, by the word of God, which liveth and abideth for ever".

Salvation by Grace

17 / The New Creation

The new creation did not get saved by his own accord or power. The new creation got saved because Jesus paid the price for his sins. The new creation is saved by grace, Ephesians 2:2–9 says that we are saved by grace through faith and not of any man's good works; it is the gift of God (Romans 5:17). Grace, which is an unmerited favour, is a divine act that translates one from the kingdom of darkness into the kingdom of His marvelous light.

The abundant Life

Christianity is a living reality. John 10:10, "I came that they may have life, and may have it abundantly." It is the abundant Life that gives healing, strength, and energy.

1Peter 5:7, "Casting all your anxiety upon Him, for He careth for you." Matthew 11:28, "Come unto me, all ye that labour and are heavy laden, and I will give you rest."

This means that in the mind of the Father there has come an end to worry, fear, and doubt. The work of the adversary has been destroyed.

Exodus 23:25–26 was given to the Jews under the First Covenant, but it may become a living, sweet reality to us: "And ye shall serve Jehovah your God, and He will bless thy bread, and thy water; and I will take sickness away from the midst of thee. There shall none cast her young, nor be barren, in thy land; the number of thy days I will fulfill."

Is our Covenant as good as that?

Philippians 4:19, "And my God shall supply every need of

yours according to His riches unveiled in Christ Jesus." (Lit trans.) Philippians 4:13, "I can do all things in Him that strengtheneth me." Philippians 4:11, "Not that I speak in respect of want: for I have learned, in whatsoever state I am, therein to be independent of circumstances." (20th Century trans.)

We rise into the realm of the supernatural, absolute overcomers, perfect victors in Christ. Is it any wonder that Paul, declares, "Nay in all these things we are more than conquerors?" (Romans 8:37) There is nothing that can separate us from the love of God as unveiled in Christ Jesus, our Lord.

Romans 8:32, "He that spared not His own Son, but delivered Him up for us all, how shall He not also with Him freely give us all things?"

We stand upon the mount of victory. Now we can say, "There is no more sickness in the body of Christ." His Word is a reality in the lives of the sons of God. We are going out today to destroy the works of the enemy in the bodies, minds, and spirits of men.

There are several methods of healing.

The one that stands first in the mind of the Spirit is found in Isaiah 53:4–6: "Surely He has borne our griefs (sicknesses, weaknesses, and distresses) and carried our sorrows and pains [of punishment], yet we [ignorantly] considered Him stricken, smitten, and afflicted by God [as if with leprosy]. But He was wounded for our transgressions, He was bruised for our guilt and iniquities;

the chastisement [needful to obtain] peace and well-being for us was upon Him, and with the stripes [that wounded] Him we are healed and made whole. All we like sheep have gone astray, we have turned every one to his own way; and the Lord has made to light upon Him the guilt and iniquity of us all." (Amplified Bible)

You are the blessed

"Blessed be the God and father of our Lord Jesus Christ Who hath blessed us with every spiritual blessing in the heavenly places in Christ." (Ephesians 1:3).

Not only are we seated in the highest position in the universe, but we are also blessed with every spiritual blessing that is necessary to maintain our place as members of His glorious body.

In the mind of God, everyone of us is in Christ now. He sees us in Him. When we go to the throne of Grace in prayer, it is as though Jesus were going there, for we go in His Name. Colossians 3:3, "For ye died, and your life is hid with Christ in God."

We are hidden from the adversary, but we are visible to the Father. Hebrews 9:24, "For Christ entered not into a holy place made with hands, like in pattern to the true; but into heaven itself, now to appear before the face of God for us." He is there at the right hand of the Father as our representative, as our Lord, as our Lover who gave Himself for us.

We can see that our Redemption is a completed, finished thing. Hebrews 10:12, "But this man, after he had offered one sacrifice for sins for ever, sat down on the right hand of God;" If Christ sat down at God's right hand, it is because the Father accepted Him and accepted what He did for us. The fact that He is seated there is the seal of our acceptance in the Beloved.

The ability of God within us

The most thrilling thing that I have ever learned about Redemption is the marvellous ability of God that is in the Believer. We have God's life in us.

"Wherefore if any man is in Christ, he is a new creation: the old things are passed away; behold, they are become new." (2Corinthians 5:17). Notice carefully that the believer is a New Creation. He is created in Christ Jesus. He is the workmanship of God. This New Creation has become a reality to him because he has received the life and nature of God. 1John 5:13 "These things I have written unto you, that ye may know that ye have eternal life, even unto you that believe on the name of the Son of God."

You can see now that you have within you, as you read this, if you are His child, the life and nature of God. 2Peter 1:4 tells us that we have become partakers of the divine nature. "Whereby he hath granted unto us his precious and exceeding great promises; that by these ye may become partakers of the divine nature, having escaped from the corruption thas is in the world by lust." Jesus emphasizes this by His illustration, "I am the vine, ye are the branches." (John 15:5).

The object of His coming was that we might have life, and have it abundantly. John 10:10 "I came that they may have life, and may have it abundantly." You have received Eternal life. The Eternal Life is the nature of the Father as unveiled in Christ. John 5:24 "Verily, verily, I say unto you, He that heareth my word, and believeth on him that sent me, hath everlasting life, and shall not come into condemnation; but is passed from death unto life."

As a branch of the vine, the same life that is manifested in the vine is flowing out through you and bearing fruit. It is the vine's life in you that produces fruitage of love, of faith, and of joy.

Let God's Word abide in you

John 15:7 "If ye abide in me, and my words abide in you, ye shall ask what ye will, and it shall be done unto you." Colossians 3:16 "Let the word of Christ dwell in you richly"

What is it doing there? It is admonishing, it is educating, it is training, it is correcting, it is building faith and love into your spirit.

Acts 20:32 "Now I commend you to God, and to the word of his grace, which is able to build you up, and to give you the inheritance among all them that are sanctified." It is the Word that builds you up. It is the Word that makes you know of your inheritance. It is the Word that unveils to you your relationship to the Father-God. It is the Word that makes you know your rights and privileges in Christ.

You remember it was the words of Christ that healed most of the people who came to Him. He said they were His Father's words. The Pauline Revelation is the Father's words about Jesus.

When you say you are a New Creation created in Christ, the Father's words are expressing a fact through your lips. When you say, "In the Name of Jesus, disease, stop being," you are using the Father's words that He spoke through Jesus' lips. When you step out into your rights of Righteousness and begin to bear fruit, it will be the same kind of fruit Jesus bore in His earthly walk.

Righteousness means the ability to stand in the Father's presence without the sense of guilt or inferiority. This Righteousness become yours through the finished work of Jesus Christ. Romans 4:25 "Who was delivered up for our trespasses, and was raised for our justification." He died for our sins and his resurrection gives us righteousness.

Who is man?

Man is a spirit; he has a soul and lives in a body. 1Thessalonians 5:23, "And the very God of peace sanctify you wholly; and I pray God your whole spirit and soul and body be preserved blameless unto the coming of our Lord Jesus Christ." Hebrews 4:12, "For the word of God is quick, and powerful, and sharper than any twoedged sword, piercing even to the dividing asunder of soul and spirit, and of the joints and marrow, and is a discerner of the thoughts and intents of the heart." Job 10:11, "Thou hast clothed me with skin and flesh, and hast fenced me with bones and sinews."

These scriptures confirm that man is a spirit; he has a soul and lives in a body. The spirit man is that 'being' that communes with and responds to God by the agency of the Holy Spirit. The spirit gives life to the body and could have dominion over the soul and body. The spirit of man is ageless, and has a voice, which is his conscience.

It is the spirit man who got saved. "Therefore, if any man (spirit) be in Christ, he is a new creature, old things have passed away, behold all things are become new." (2Corinthians 5:17). The human spirit is created anew in Christ Jesus. 1Corinthians 6:17, "But he that is joined unto the Lord is one spirit."

"And I will pray the Father, and he shall give you another Comforter, that he may abide with you for ever" (John 14:16).

You have the Holy Spirit in you

Jesus promised the disciples that the Holy Spirit, who was with them, should be in them. On the day of Pentecost, after He had recreated them, He entered into their bodies.

What a miracle it is to have God in us. It is wonderful to have His Word abiding in us when we realize that the universe has been created by His Word, and we have that creative ability in us. Now we have God Himself in us, along with His Word. No wonder He said in 1John 4:4: "Ye are of God, my little children, and have overcome them: because greater is he that is in you than he that is in the world."

The God in us is the same God who spoke a universe into being. The same God is in us who walked the sea in Galilee. The same God is in us who arose from the dead. Philippians 2:13 "For it is God who is at work within you."

We have not taken advantage of the riches of grace that belong to us. How few of us have let God loose in us. I can feel Him struggling to have His place and to have His rights in the individual members of the body of Christ.

How He longs to heal the sick, to break the power of Satan over the lives of men through us.

Let us let Him loose in us.

Recreation of the human spirit

This is the solution of the human problem: God giving His Nature and His Love to fallen man.

He is no longer a fallen man. He is a New Creation man united with Jesus Christ, the Head of the New Creation. He is the "raised together with Christ" man.

Ephesians 2:4–6, "But God, who is rich in mercy, for his great love wherewith he loved us, Even when we were dead in sins, hath quickened us together with Christ, (by grace ye are saved;) And hath raised us up together, and made us sit together in heavenly places in Christ Jesus:" 2Corinthians 5:17, "Wherefore if any man is in Christ, he is a new creature: the old things are passed away; behold they are become new."

His old sin consciousness, his old fallen life, his old sin life, and his old evil habits that grew out of Spiritual Death have passed away. 1John 3:14, "We know that we have passed from death unto life, because we love the brethren. He that loveth not his brother abideth in death."

He is a New Creation. He is a New Being. The Father has no memory of his past life. He is a new-born babe. His old past life has stopped being in the Mind of Justice and in the Mind of the Father.

A New Creation has come into being through grace. 2Corinthians 5:18, "But all these things are of God, who reconciled us to himself through Christ Jesus, and gave unto us the ministry of reconciliation."

Amplified Bible states it: "But all these things are from God, who reconciled us to Himself through Christ [making us acceptable to Him] and gave us the ministry of reconciliation [so that by our example we might bring others to Him],"

Look at it again. He has given us through Christ the ministry of reconciliation – not a ministry of condemnation which we have had for the last hundred years, but a ministry of reconciliation.

We have been reminding men of their sins. We have kept them under sin consciousness. We have kept them conscious of their weaknesses and failings.

We have preached sin instead of Eternal Life. We have preached judgement instead of reconciliation, when God has committed unto us the "word of reconciliation."

We have that Word. We have that message. It is ours to give to the world.

We have become New Creations. We have been recreated by Love. Love has been imparted to our spirit beings.

God is Love and God's Nature is Love; but God is also Life, the Author of Life. So He has imparted to us His Life Nature, His Love Nature. God has imparted His Nature to us, making us New Creations. That Nature is Righteousness. It is Holiness. It is Reality. It is Love. It has been imparted to us. We are ambassadors on behalf of Christ, and we are entreating the world to be reconciled to God.

Why? Because "Him who knew no sin God made to become sin that we might become the righteousness of God in him." God made Jesus sin to the end that He could make us righteous through the New Creation.

We have become New Creations. We have also become the "righteousness of God in him."

2Corinthians 5:19–21, "To wit, that God was in Christ, reconciling the world unto himself, not imputing their trespasses unto them; and hath committed unto us the word of reconciliation. Now then we are ambassadors for Christ, as though God did beseech you by us: we pray you in Christ's stead, be ye reconciled to God. For he hath made him to be sin for us, who knew no sin; that we might be made the righteousness of God in him."

We have a reconciling message of love to give to the world. It is not a message of condemnation but of reconciliation; not of judgement, but of love.

Jesus was made sin, was judged, and suffered all that we would have suffered had we rejected Him. By our acceptance of Him we enter into all that He purchased for us.

This message is not an appeal to human reason or Sense Knowledge. It is the Father's appeal to our spirits. We ought to understand that the Father does not reveal Himself to our reasoning faculties but to our spirits. Our reasoning faculties can only apprehend the things that the Five Senses convey to them. Outside of that, the reasoning faculties are dumb and unfruitful.

When our spirits are recreated they receive Eternal Life. We can know the Father. We can enjoy fellowship with Him through His Word. We have become so utterly identified with Him, so utterly one with Him that the "Vine and the Branch" is the only suitable illustration of this new and beautiful relationship. We are a part of the Vine life. We are bearing the love fruit of the Vine life.

Our spirits enjoy the reality of Christ in the Word. Our

minds may not be able to grasp it; but if we let our minds be renewed by acting on the Word and meditating in it, our minds and spirits will come into sweet fellowship with each other.

The recreated human spirit never grows old. It has received Eternal Life. It has become one with the Father.

Ephesians 5:30, "For we are members of his body, of his flesh, and of his bones." Our bodies will grow old. Our minds will grow old because they derive all their knowledge from the body.

If our spirits can gain the ascendancy over our bodies, they will keep our minds from aging, and our bodies in a vigorous, healthy, youthful condition.

Sense Knowledge wanes with the senility of the senses. The senses will wear out and lose their freshness and beauty unless they are renewed by a recreated spirit.

The development of our recreated spirits comes by meditating in the Word, acting on the Word, and letting the Word live in us and become a part of us.

The new creation lives on the word of God. 1Peter 2:2, "As newborn babes, desire the sincere milk of the word, that ye may grow thereby:" Matthew 4:4, "It is written, Man shall not live by bread alone, but by every word that proceedeth out of the mouth of God."

The word is the meal for the spirit wherein it derives its nourishment to grow and attain fullness in Christ.

Hebrews 5:12–14, "For when for the time ye ought to be teachers, ye have need that one teach you again which be the first principles of the oracles of God; and are become such as have need of milk, and not of strong meat. For every one that useth milk is unskilful in the word of righteousness: for he is a babe. But strong meat belongeth to them that are of full age, even those who by reason of use have their senses exercised to discern both good and evil."

The fruit of the created human spirit

The new creation has the nature of God imparted into his spirit. Hence the new creation has the character of God in him that he exhibits as the fruit of the recreated spirit: love, joy, peace, long-suffering, gentleness, goodness, faith, meekness, and temperance (Galatians 5:22).

The soul of man

The soul houses the mind, the emotion and the intellect or the will.

1. The mind (Luke 9:47) is the part of the soul that thinks. A man's thought is as powerful as his action and word and therefore can control your body and affect its discipline.

2. The will is the part of the soul that makes decision.

3. The emotion of man has to do with his feeling.

The soul is the doorway to the spirit; as such if the mind (soul) of a man is blocked, his spirit becomes inaccessible. The soul has control over the body. It is where a man carries out his reasoning and his recording system.

The renewal of the mind

The renewal of the mind is a sanctification that is continual for the new creation. Our minds need to be renewed (discard the old thoughts and intents and be filled with the knowledge of His will) that we may know the mind of Christ and Walk in His will. Romans 12:1–3, "I beseech you therefore, brethren, by the mercies of God, that ye present your bodies a living sacrifice, holy, acceptable unto God, which is your reasonable service. And be not conformed to this world: but be ye transformed by the renewing of your mind, that ye may prove what is that good, and acceptable, and perfect, will of God. For I say, through the grace given unto me, to every man that is among you, not to think of himself more highly than he ought to think; but to think soberly, according as God hath dealt to every man the measure of faith."

Renewal of mind brings total transformation to the new creation. Ephesians 4:22–24, "That ye put off concerning the former conversation the old man, which is corrupt according to the deceitful lusts; And be renewed in the spirit of your mind; And that ye put on the new man, which after God is created in righteousness and true holiness."

Sanctifying the thoughts

Temptation does not come from God, it is self contrived by reason of man's lustful thought, which gives birth to sin and death.

James 1:13–15, "Let no man say when he is tempted, I am tempted of God: for God cannot be tempted with evil, neither tempteth he any man: But every man is tempted, when he is drawn away of his own lust, and enticed. Then when lust hath conceived, it bringeth forth sin: and sin, when it is finished, bringeth forth death."

It originates only because our thoughts gave birth to it. Hence, cleansing the thoughts keeps the right intents in the heart.

Renewed by the word of God

The new creation is transformed by the word, as we meditate on the word of God we become like Him and exactly what His word says we are, by the transforming power of God's word. 2Corinthians 3:18 says, "but we all with open face beholding as in a glass the glory of the Lord are changed into the same image from glory to glory, even as by the Spirit of the Lord".

The body and its discipline

The body is the covering of the spirit man (Job 10:11). It's with his body that a man attends to daily life issues. The body like all other perishable things that exist on earth is limited by time. The body also gives man the legal right to exist and function here on earth.

Now that the new creation is alive in Christ, and has a renewed mind by the word of God, there is need to discipline (domesticate) the body. 1Corinthians 9:24–27, "Know ye not that they which run in a race run all, but one receiveth the prize? So run, that ye may obtain. And every man that striveth for the mastery is temperate in all things. Now they do it to obtain a corruptible crown; but we an incorruptible. I therefore so run, not as uncertainly; so fight I, not as one that beateth the air: But I keep under my body, and bring it into subjection: lest that by any means, when I have preached to others, I myself should be a castaway."

Apostle Paul tells us that conscious effort has to be made by the new creation to discipline his body, that is to bring his body under subjection that he may fulfill the purpose of his life. Colossians 3:5, "Mortify therefore your members which are upon the earth; fornication, uncleanness, inordinate affection, evil concupiscence, and covetousness, which is idolatry:"

Romans 6:13–15, "Neither yield ye your members as instruments of unrighteousness unto sin: but yield yourselves unto God, as those that are alive from the dead, and your members as instruments of righteousness unto God. For sin shall not have dominion over you: for ye are not un-der the law, but under grace. What then? shall we sin, because we are not under the law, but under grace? God forbid."

You are translated

The new creation was translated from darkness (ignorance) into light (knowledge). The new creation is conscious of the realm in which he lives (Colossians 1:13).

At salvation, you are translated into the kingdom of God. Colossians 1:13 "Who hath delivered us from the power of darkness, and hath translated us into the kingdom of his dear Son"

In the kingdom of darkness, there are all forms of evil. All manner of sicknesses, afflictions, embarrassments, torments and bad luck, hold sway in this kingdom of darkness. The inhabitants have no source of help, as long as they continue dwelling therein. They are ruled and governed by the devil.

The Bible calls them the children of disobedience, and the devil continually lords it over them. They can not protest. They have no right to. Their will has been submitted to the devil. They are servants of sin. (Romans 6:16) held in bondage by the devil.

But you are no longer under the devil domain, so he has no more control over you or your affairs. The blood of Jesus, shed on the cross of Calvary, has delivered you from that realm and translated you into the kingdom of God Himself.

You have been brought out of darkness into light. You have become a partaker of the life and nature of the Father God (2Peter 1:4). The highest class there is, is God and His family. This is where you now belong.

I would like you to be aware of the beauty of this translation. The essence of Christianity borders on it. Until you experience it, you remain terrestrial and everything that functions here on earth will work against you and destroy you. Seek to experience your translated position. t works! Satan has no access at all to this kingdom unto which you have been translated. It is the kingdom of light. There is no place for him there, because he is 'the darkness'. That is why God said to us that wherever we find him operating, we should cast him out (Mark 16:17). Friend, it one thing for you to be translated, and another thing for you to be aware that you have been translated. May the Lord give you understanding.

The word of God confirms that we are the children of God by reason of our confession and belief.

Romans 10:9–11, "That if thou shalt confess with thy mouth the Lord Jesus, and shalt believe in thine heart that God hath raised him from the dead, thou shalt be saved. For with the heart man believeth unto righteousness; and with the mouth confession is made unto salvation. For the scripture saith, Whosoever believeth on him shall not be ashamed.

" Matthew 12:37 says, "for by thy words thou shalt be justified…"

1John 5:9–13, "If we receive the witness of men, the witness of God is greater: for this is the witness of God which he hath testified of his Son. He that believeth on the

Son of God hath the witness in himself: he that believeth not God hath made him a liar; because he believeth not the record that God gave of his Son. And this is the record, that God hath given to us eternal life, and this life is in his Son. He that hath the Son hath life; and he that hath not the Son of God hath not life. These things have I written unto you that believe on the name of the Son of God; that ye may know that ye have eternal life, and that ye may believe on the name of the Son of God."

The Holy Spirit bears witness with our spirit that we are the children (sons) of God. (Romans 8:16).

Remission for the unsaved

Matthew 26:28, "For this is my blood of the new testament, which is shed for many for the remission of sins."

Acts 2:38, "Then Peter said unto them, Repent, and be baptized every one of you in the name of Jesus Christ for the remission of sins, and ye shall receive the gift of the Holy Ghost."

In Ephesians 1:7, Paul explains "we have redemption through His blood, the forgiveness of sins, according to the riches of His grace".

The scripture says that remission, washing away of sin or blotting out of sin, is for the unregenerate i.e. The unsaved. This is necessary for them to become part of the commonwealth of God's children in Christ Jesus.

Forgiveness for the Christian

1John 1:9–10, "If we confess our sins, He is faithful and just to forgive us our sins, and to cleanse us from all unrighteousness. If we say that we have not sinned, we make him a liar, and his Word is not in us."

The Christian belongs to God and has the grace of God that ensures his citizenship of the commonwealth of God's people. When he commits sin he has an advocate with the father, Jesus Christ the righteous.

1John 2:1–3, "My little children, these things write I unto you, that ye sin not. And if any man sin, we have an advocate with the Father, Jesus Christ the righteous: And he is the propitiation for our sins: and not for ours only, but also for the sins of the whole world. And hereby we do know that we know him, if we keep his commandments."

The word "Propitiare" is Latin and means to appease. Hence propitiation means that which appeases. Jesus is the propitiation for our sins. This means He, Himself, is the sacrifice which atones for your sins.

The new creation has power of God to live above sin by the help of the Holy Spirit that is at work in us. He also has the grace to ask for forgiveness if he does sin. However, the word of God does not encourage sin, rather it builds and strengthens the inner man (new creation) to live and enjoy a glorious life in Christ.

Conclusion

37 / The New Creation

2Corinthians 5:17 says, "Therefore if any man be in Christ, he is a new creature: old things are passed away; behold, all things are become new."

Behold means to see! See, you are a new creature! You are ambassadors for Christ! You have eternal life! (1John 5:13) You are of God! (1John 4:4) You have overcome them! Greater is He that is in you, than he that is in the world! As 1John 4:17 says, "as he is, so are we in this world."

1Peter 2:9 says, you are "a chosen generation", you are "a

NEW CREATION / 38

Chapter 2

WHO THE CHRISTIAN REALLY IS

royal priesthood", you are "an holy nation", you are "a peculiar people";

You are unique, special people! You are "out of darkness". You are "into his marvellous light"!

"If any man be in Christ he is a new creature . . . " (2Corinthians5:17). This new creature, the Christian, has the life and nature of God. The new birth means he is born of God and therefore belongs to God's family. As a new creature, he never existed before, he is a new being, which is born not of blood, nor of the will of the flesh, nor of man, but of God.

We are united with the Father and Son Jesus

Christianity is a relationship between the Father and His family. God the father, Jesus, and You. John 14:20, "At that day ye shall know that I am in my Father, and ye in me, and I in you."

It is not a religion. It is not having your sins forgiven. It is not joining the church.

It is being made a New Creation in Christ. It is being born from above. It is receiving the Nature and Life of God. It is being united with Christ.

Romans 6:5, "For if we have become united with him in the likeness of death, we shall be also in the likeness of his resurrection." We are united with Him in Resurrection Life.

The New Creation is to enjoy the dominion that Adam lost in the fall. In Ezekiel 36:26,27 He speaks out His heart's dream: "A new heart also will I give you, and a new spirit will I put within you; and I will take away the stony heart out of your flesh, and I will give you a heart of flesh. And I will put my spirit within you, and cause you to walk in my statutes, and you shall keep mine ordinances, and do them."

Man was to have a new heart. That means that his heart was to be recreated. When the Lord speaks of the heart, He means the spirit, the real man.

The New Creation is the outstanding miracle of Redemption. On the day of Pentecost when the Spirit recreated one hundred and twenty in the upper room, God began the "New Thing."

They had more than forgiveness of sin. They had new

41 / Who The Christian Really Is

Natures. It was the union of Love with man.

God is Love. God's Nature becomes man's nature. Man becomes a lover.

It is a new order of things. 2Corinthians 5:17, "Therefore if any man is in Christ, there is a New Creation." They are a new species, new lovers.

The expression, "Newcreation," means a newthing, something unheard of before. This new man was an unknown thing just as the first Adam was an unknown being. This new love nature means that the old order of selfishness is ended and that the new love life is begun.

The New Creation is a God-man, born of heaven. He is like the sample, Jesus. He is God's superman. He is to walk in the realm of the supernatural. He is to be ruled by the Lord. He has been ruled by Satan.

He is called in Hebrews 10:38 the Righteous one, the God-made one. "My righteous one shall walk by faith." He is the new love man ruled by our love-Lord, Jesus. He was by nature a child of wrath. He is by the new Nature a child of God.

The God Who created man in the beginning is recreating man now. John 3:3–8 says that the recreated man is born from above: "Jesus answered and said unto him, Verily, verily, I say unto thee: except a man be born again, he cannot see the kingdom of God. Nicodemus saith unto him, How can a man be born when he is old? Can he enter the second time into his mother's womb and be born?

Jesus answered, Verily, verily, I say unto you, except a man be born of water and the Spirit, he cannot enter into the kingdom of God. That which is born of the flesh is flesh; and that which is born of the Spirit is spirit. Marvel not that I said unto thee, Ye must be born again. The wind bloweth where it listeth and thou hearest the sound thereof, but canst not tell whence it cometh and whither it goeth: so is every one that is born of the Spirit."

He is born of the Word and of the Spirit. Read these verses carefully and you will notice that he is recreated by the will of the Father.

He is a wanted child. James 1:18, "Of his own will he brought us forth by the Word of truth."

We are recreated by the Spirit through the Word. 1Peter 1:23, "Having been begotten again, not of corruptible seed, but of incorruptible, through the Word of God, which liveth and abideth."

No man recreates himself. It is purely the work of God. The only part we have in it is to consent to God's giving us His Nature and to recognize the Lordship of the new Head of the New Creation, Jesus. Ephesians 2:8–9, "For by grace have ye been saved through faith; and that not of yourselves, it is the gift of God; not of works, that no man should glory.

"Ephesians 2:10, "We are His workmanship created in Christ Jesus." When you know that you have been recreated by God Himself, you know that the work is satisfactory to the Author of the work. It gives you a real foundation for faith.

Our chief difficulty has been the sense of unworthiness which has robbed us of faith and fellowship with the Father. This is due to our ignorance of what we are in Christ and of what the New Birth means to the Father and may mean to us.

Ephesians 4:24, "Put on the newman that after God hath been created in righteousness and holiness of truth."

We are created in Righteousness. We are created out of the very Nature and Heart of the Father; so that when He declares that we are created of Righteousness and Holiness, and of reality (or Truth), we know that we can stand before the Father without any sense of guilt or sin. We know that this New Creation is the Righteousness of God in Christ.

1 John 5:13, "These things have I written unto you, that ye may know that ye have eternal life, even unto you that believe on the name of the Son of God." So then Eternal Life is received in Jesus' Name.

Romans 8:14–17 is the climax of Redemption as outlined in this Epistle: "For as many as are led by the Spirit of God, these are sons of God. For ye received not the spirit of bondage again unto fear; but ye received the spirit of adoption, whereby we cry, Abba, Father. The Spirit himself beareth witness with our spirit, that we are children of God: and if children, then heirs; heirs of God, and joint-heirs with Christ."

1 John 3:1–2, "Behold, what manner of love the Father hath

bestowed upon us, that we should be called the sons of God: therefore the world knoweth us not, because it knew him not. Beloved, now are we the sons of God, and it doth not yet appear what we shall be: but we know that, when he shall appear, we shall be like him; for we shall see him as he is."

This is the climax of Redemption. This is the objective toward which God was working: to bring man into the actual relationship of a son through his partaking of God's Nature, Eternal Life.

Galatians 4:5–7, "That He might redeem them that are under the law, that we (Jews) might receive the adoption of sons. And because ye are sons, God sent forth the Spirit of his Son into our hearts, crying, Abba, Father. So that thou art no longer a bondservant, but a son; and if a son, then an heir through God."

The Jews were the servants of God; we are the sons of God. 1John 3:2, "Beloved, now are we the sons of God." 2Corinthians 5:21, "Him who knew no sin He made to be sin on our behalf; that we might become the righteousness of God in him." John 1:13, "Who were born, not of blood, nor of the will of the flesh, nor of the will of man, but of God."

This should forever settle the question of whether there is anything that an unsaved man can do to give himself the New Birth outside of his acceptance of Christ as Savior and Lord. All of his crying, weeping, repenting, and confessing of sins has no bearing upon it whatever.

This is hard work for us to accept because we have been ruled by the teaching of the Dark Ages – the teaching of works. The church is under bondage today, to the Grecian philosophy and the Christianity that we find during the Middle Ages.

All that Luther saw was Justification by Faith. He had no clear conception of a New Birth, of righteousness, of God as a Father, or of our place as sons and daughters of God. He saw it vaguely. He saw one truth. That one truth brought him out of bondage and gave to Germany a new civilization.

1John 5:1, "Whosoever believeth that Jesus is the Christ is begotten of God." 1John 5:4–5, "For whatsoever is born of God overcometh the world: and this is the victory that overcometh the world, even our faith. Who is he that overcometh the world, but he that believeth that Jesus is the Son of God?"

The fourth verse reads, for whatsoever is born of God overcometh the world; and this is the victory that hath overcome the world, even our faith.

The New Creation is an overcomer.

You are a New Creation

By virtue of Christ's redemptive work, you have become a new creation, if you have accepted Jesus as your Lord and Saviour. This new status grants you entrance into God's class.

Because you are born again, you have become a completely new creation, Brand new! Not an adjustment of your old self, not a modification of an old status. 2Corinthians 5:17 "Therefore, if any man be in christ, he is a new creature: old things are passed away; behold, all things have become new."

By this you have become accepted by the beloved, the family of God the father. God declares your righteousness, he becomes your real father, and you become his real son (John 1:12). He comes into you with all His strength, glory and majesty, and makes you strong in Him.

You are God's offspring. You are His beloved son. You occupy a special space in His heart. You have His nature, His life, His sprit, His faith, His love (Ezekiel 36:29). Everything God is and has, is now made available to you (Ephesians 2:4–6).

You have become one with Christ. You are joined with Him. What you lost in Adam in the beginning, you have regained in Christ. You are now restored to your former place of authority and dominion. You can now hold sway over every situation in life, by virtue of your new class of being. You are as invincible, as indestructible as God. No devil can defeat you as you stand in your proper position in God. The nature of God is now yours personally. You have been declared more than a conqueror.

God took you out of the powers and kingdom of the devil, and translated you into the kingdom of the Son of His love. This is a mystery. But it is the truth and is real.

You are no longer that person who it was so cheap for the devil to cheat, oppress and afflict. Now you can boldly say to him, "Satan, get out!"

Born into God's family

Once a person accepts Jesus Christ as his Lord and saviour, he is immediately translated from the kingdom of darkness into the kingdom of God. Colossians 1:12–13, "Giving thanks unto the Father, which hath made us meet to be partakers of the inheritance of the saints in light: Who hath delivered us from the power of darkness, and hath translated us into the kingdom of his dear Son:" Once you've been translated into Gods kingdom you become a member of his family and all members of the family of God live in the kingdom of God.

Paul speaking in Ephesians 3:14–15 makes it clear that the members of the family of God reside in heaven and on earth: "For this cause I bow my knees unto the Father of our Lord Jesus Christ, Of whom the whole family in heaven and earth is named," As Christians we are members of the family of God resident on earth.

The New Creation is born of God

John 1:11–14 puts it succinctly that once we receive Jesus by believing the gospel we are given the power to become sons of God: "He came unto his own, and his own received him not. But as many as received him, to them gave he power to become the sons of God, even to them that believe on his name: Which were born, not of blood, nor of the will of the flesh, nor of the will of man, but of God. And the Word was made flesh, and dwelt among us, (and we beheld his glory, the glory as of the only begotten of the Father,) full of grace and truth."

Not children born of blood, nor flesh, nor of the will of man but of God.

1Peter 1:23 (New Living Translation), "For you have been born again, but not to a life that will quickly end. Your new life will last forever because it comes from the eternal, living word of God."

For you have been born again. Your new life did not come from your earthly parents because the life they gave you will end in death.

Hebrews 12:9, "Furthermore we have had fathers of our flesh which corrected us, and we gave them reverence: shall we not much rather be in subjection unto the Father of spirits, and live?"

This new life will last forever because it comes from the eternal, living word of God.

Ephesians 4:6, "One God and Father of all, who is above all, and through all, and in you all."

Furthermore, the Bible refers to Jesus Christ in John 3:16 and John 1:14 as the "only begotten Son" of God. Is this true?

Yes and No. Now as at that time, Jesus *was* the only begotten of the father but *after* the Pentecost when the Holy

Ghost descended, Jesus *ceased* to be the *only* begotten of the father but he became the *first* begotten of the father. Hebrews 1:6, "And again, when He bringeth in the *firstbegotten* into the world, He saith, And let all the angels of God worship Him."

Hebrews 12:22-23, "But ye are come unto mount Sion, and unto the city of the living God, the heavenly Jerusalem, and to an innumerable company of angels, To the general assembly and *church of the firstborn*, which are written in heaven, and to God the Judge of all, and to the spirits of just men made perfect,"

Apostle Paul refers to Jesus as the "firstbegotten" and the "firstborn".

Apostle Peter mentions that "the God and Father of our Lord Jesus Christ" has "begotten us again" (1Peter 1:3).

Also Apostle John himself, in 1John 5:1, "Whosoever believeth that Jesus is the Christ is born of God: and every one that loveth Him that begat loveth him also that is begotten of Him."

You are peculiar

Every cleansed person is a peculiar treasure! You are not common! Acts 10:15, "What God hath cleansed, that call not thou common."

You're bought with a price – the precious blood of the lamb. You belong to royalty, you're the holiness of God, chosen to show forth the praises of God on earth.

You are peculiar! Different! To be envied! Strange! A special breed!

"But ye are a chosen generation, a royal priesthood, an holy nation, a peculiar people; that ye should shew forth the praises of him who hath called you out of darkness into his marvelous light: Which in time past were not a people, but are now the people of God" (1Peter 2:9–10).

Now your ways are past finding out! John 3:8, "The wind bloweth where it listeth, and thou hearest the sound thereof, but canst not tell whence it cometh, and whither it goeth: so is every one that is born of the Spirit."

You're a sign and a wonder! Decked in God holiness! Showing forth His glory on the earth. But, if you don't know all these, you will live and die like mere men!

Look, sickness should see you and run, if you understand your peculiarity in God. You were not created to be tossed about by every evil wind of Satan.

So, have dominion!

Dominion means rulership, control, authority, and mastership. As a Christian you have control or authority over the following.

You have dominion over the world

The Bible refers to the devil as the god of this world. 2Corinthians 4:4, "In whom the god of this world hath blinded the minds of them which believe not, lest the light of the glorious gospel of Christ, who is the image of God, should shine unto them."

However Jesus spoiled principalities and powers (the devils) and made a show of them openly, triumphing over them in it (Colossians 2:15).

Now from the above, though the devil is the god of this world, Jesus has defeated him. The bible says in Ephesians 3:17 that Christ dwells in our heart by faith and therefore it is expressly declared in the book of 1John 4:4 that we are of God and that greater is he (Christ) that is in us than he that is in the world.

1John 5:4, "For whatsoever is born of God overcometh the world: and this is the victory that overcometh the world, even our faith."

Whatsoever is born of God overcomes the world. If you are born of God, you overcome the world!

1John 4:4, "You, dear children, are from God and have overcome them, because the one who is in you is greater than the one who is in the world."

You have dominion over life circumstances

Romans 5:17 states thus: "For if by one man's offence death reigned by one; much more they who receive abundance of Grace and of the gift of Righteousness shall reign in life by one Jesus Christ".

Through Christ's obedience from the things he suffered, he became the source of eternal salvation and man received the ability to reign in all circumstances.

You have dominion over sin

Romans 6:14, "For sin shall not have dominion over you, for you are not under the law but under the Grace".

Now how did sin come? Romans 7:8, "But sin, taking occasion by the commandment, wrought in me all manner of concupiscence. For without the law sin was dead".

So sin came through the law, but Jesus speaking in Matthew 5:17 said, "Think not that I am come to destroy the law, or the prophets: I am not come to destroy, but to fulfil".

In John 19:30, "When Jesus therefore had received the vinegar, he said, It is finished —"; marking the fulfilment of the law. So, if any man be in Christ he has fulfilled the law and therefore is not under the law; and as a result of this, sin is dead to him or he is dead to sin.

You are above all

John 3:31 says: "He that cometh from above is above all..."

By this scripture, you are above everything happening on this earth – failure, disease, sickness, poverty, depression, frustration, rejection, barrenness, miscarriage, life threats, etc.

Just think of it. Because you're from above, where you are seated with Christ (Ephesians 2:6), you are above all these things.

God's reasons for salvation

In Genesis 12:1–2, "Now the Lord had said unto Abram get thee out of thy country and from thy kindred and from thy father's house unto a land that I will show thee: And I will make thee a great nation and I will bless thee and make thy name great and you shall be a blessing".

The call of Abram can be likened to our translation from the kingdom of darkness into God's kingdom. Abram was told to leave his country and kindred where there was idol worship unto a place where God alone is to be worshiped.

God also promised to bless Abraham and make his name great. Through Christ, we have received this promise, for the bible says in Genesis 13:16, Now to Abraham and his seed was the promise made. He did not say to 'his seeds', as of many, but as of one, to thy seed: which is Christ

To be blessed is to be empowered to prosper in all things: health, wealth, relationships or friendship, etc.

Also from Genesis 12:3, God said that through thee shall all the families of the earth be blessed. Acts 1:8; Matthew 28:18–20 and Mark 16:5–20 commissions us to bless the families of the earth by preaching the Gospel.

Matthew 28:18–20, "And Jesus came and spake unto them, saying, All power is given unto me in heaven and in earth.

Go ye therefore, and teach all nations, baptizing them in the name of the Father, and of the Son, and of the Holy Ghost: Teaching them to observe all things whatsoever I have commanded you: and, lo, I am with you always, even unto the end of the world. Amen."

Acts 1:8, "But ye shall receive power, after that the Holy Ghost is come upon you: and ye shall be witnesses unto me both in Jerusalem, and in all Judaea, and in Samaria, and unto the uttermost part of the earth."

Mark 16:15, "And he said unto them, Go ye into all the world, and preach the gospel to every creature."

We are saved that we may prosper (3John 2). We are saved that we may be a source of blessing to all. We are saved that we may escape the destruction that is to come.

What is truth

John 17:17 makes us know that the word of God is truth, "Sanctify them through thy truth: thy word is truth."

Sight is anything we can perceive with our physical senses i.e. smell, touch, sight, hear, and taste.

2Corinthians 5:7, "For we walk by faith, not by sight"

Sight and truth may not always agree e.g. a Christian may have all the symptoms of malaria, but in truth he has been healed by the stripes of our Lord Jesus. Isaiah 53:5, "He was wounded for our transgressions, He was bruised for our iniquities: the chastisement of our peace was upon Him;

and with His stripes we are healed."

Jonah speaking in Jonah 2:8 said, "they that observe lying vanities forsake their own mercy". Lying vanities here refers to things that can be seen, perceived, smelt and touched, etc., but don't align with God's Word (the truth).

However it is also possible for the sight to align with Gods word e.g. a Christian full of health, wealth and wisdom.

What it means to be a Christian

That if you confess with your mouth, "Jesus is Lord," and believe in your heart that God raised him from the dead, you will be saved. For it is with your heart that you believe and are justified, and it is with your mouth that you confess and are saved (Romans 10:9–10).

Nobody can be born again until the proclamation of the Lordship of Jesus. That's where salvation comes from. To become a Christian, you have to proclaim the Lordship of Jesus over your life.

Confessing the Lordship of Jesus Christ is so vital because that is what gives Him the right over your life. Until you confess Jesus as Lord of your life, you are a rebel and that is the reason He has the right to cast such a person into the lake of fire. But thank God we are not rebels, because we have accepted and confessed His Lordship over our lives.

This is what being a Christian signifies. When you give your heart to Christ and say Jesus is Lord of your life, it means that you have given Jesus the authority over your life and he has become your shepherd, your Jehovah, your bread provider who takes care of you!

It doesn't stop there. It also means that He has given you His life and made you a joint-heir with Him and a partaker of His divine nature.

This is what it means to be a Christian, and this is why you must preach the gospel so that others can proclaim Jesus as Lord and receive the glorious Life that is in Him.

Christ came to give Life to man, to recreate man and give him the dominion that he lost. So, as many as accept Him, accept his provision of recreation. The outward man that was formed does not get born again, he still looks the same, but inwardly he is a new creation.

You are a son of God

1John 3:1–3, "Behold, what manner of love the Father hath bestowed upon us, that we should be called the sons of God: therefore the world knoweth us not, because it knew him not. Beloved, now are we the sons of God, and it doth not yet appear what we shall be: but we know that, when he shall appear, we shall be like him; for we shall see him as he is. And every man that hath this hope in him purifieth himself, even as he is pure."

The book of John 1:12–13 states clearly that we are empowered unto sonship once we receive Christ by accepting the gospel: "But as many as received him, to them gave he power to become the sons of God, even to them that believe on his name: Which were born, not of blood, nor of the will of the flesh, nor of the will of man, but of God."

The Holy Spirit confirms this: "The Spirit itself beareth witness with our spirit, that we are the children of God: And if children, then heirs; heirs of God, and joint-heirs with Christ; if so be that we suffer with him, that we may be also glorified together." (Romans 8:16–17).

You are a citizen of Zion

"The LORD loves the gates of Zion more than all the dwellings of Jacob. Glorious things are said of you, O city of God. Selah" (Psalms 87:2–3).

The Church of Jesus Christ is called the city of God. The Bible refers to it as Zion, the city of the great king (Psalms 48:2). Colossians 1:13, "Who hath delivered us from the power of darkness, and hath translated us into the kingdom of his dear Son:"

The Bible states clearly in Hebrews 12:22–23, "But you have come to Mount Zion, to the heavenly Jerusalem, the city of the living God. You have come to thousands upon thousands of angels in joyful assembly, to the church of the firstborn, whose names are written in heaven..."

If you are born again, you are a citizen of Zion; and as a citizen of Zion, you live above sickness and disease. The Bible says, "And the inhabitant shall not say I am sick..." (Isaiah 33:24).

The inhabitants of Zion don't fall sick because their lives don't come from blood but from the Word of God. John 17:14, "I have given them thy word; and the world hath hated them, because they are not of the world, even as I am not of the world."

Also, as a citizen of Zion, you function as a king and as a priest: "But ye are a chosen generation, a royal priesthood, an holy nation, a peculiar people" (1Peter 2:9). You minister to God as a priest (Hebrews 8:3) and declare words of power as a king (Ecclesiastes 8:4).

God has ordained every citizen of Zion to a victorious life in the earth. Some Christians don't understand this because they think Zion refers to Heaven.

No, Zion doesn't refer to Heaven. Heaven is actually a geographical location in Zion. That's why you need to understand that the gospel of Jesus Christ is not all about going to Heaven; it's about the whole kingdom of God from earth to heaven.

You are in the place of power

Ephesians 1:19–20, "And what is the exceeding greatness of his power to us-ward who believe, according to the working of his mighty power, Which he wrought in Christ, when he raised him from the dead, and set him at his own right hand in the heavenly places, Far above all principality, and power, and might, and dominion, and every name that is named, not only in this world, but also in that which is to come:"

Pay special attention to verse 20, "which he wrought in Christ when he raised him from the dead and set him at his own right hand in heavenly places, far above principalities and powers, might and dominion".

Ephesians 2:6 says, "And has raised us up together and made us sit together in heavenly places in Christ Jesus". From these, it is evident that we are seated where Christ is seated – a place of power.

Matthew 28:18, "And Jesus came and spake unto them, saying, All power is given unto me in heaven and in earth." Mark 16:17–18, "And these signs shall follow them that believe; In my name shall they cast out devils; they shall speak with new tongues; They shall take up serpents; and if they drink any deadly thing, it shall not hurt them; they shall lay hands on the sick, and they shall recover."

Ephesians 2:10, "For we are his workmanship, created in Christ Jesus unto good works, which God hath before ordained that we should walk in them."

Mark 16:16, "He that believeth and is baptized shall be saved; but he that believeth not shall be damned." Matthew 28:19, "Go ye therefore, and teach all nations, bap-tizing them in the name of the Father, and of the Son, and of the Holy Ghost."

I can do mentality

Philippians 4:13 states "I can do all things through Christ that strengthens me". The word Christ here does not refer to Jesus but rather to the Holy Spirit, the anointing.

In John 1:12–13 it is seen that we've received power to live as sons of God. 2Peter 1:3 says "according as His divine power hath given unto us all things that pertains to life and godliness through the knowledge of Him that has called us unto glory and virtue".

The power to do all things has been given to us. Mark 11:24, "Therefore I say unto you, What things soever ye desire, when ye pray, believe that ye receive them, and ye shall have them." Matthew 19:26, "Jesus beheld them, and said unto them, With men this is impossible; but with God all things are possible.

" Therefore what we need to know is how to make use of this power from the Scripture above.

In order to make use or take advantage of the power, we have to grow in the Knowledge of the Word.

You are a winner

There an innate victory mentality in your new nature. God nature is contrary to defeat and failure. He cannot fail! He doesn't have a sense of it. It is not possible with Him! God does not know failure.

You are God son, produced after His kind. So you're in His class. You're a god here on earth, Psalms 82:6, "I have said, Ye are gods; and all of you are children of the most High." You are a born winner!

By virtue of your new birth, you have been declared a winner. You have a winner covenant with God your Father. He has destined you to win. You are no meant for failure and defeat, but for great exploits in victory.

There is no fight, however fierce, no battle however tough, that you cannot win! You can have as many victories as the battles you have, as long as you abide in God and know Him intimately. Your degree of exploits becomes unlimited. There is no limit to what God will do to give you victory over Satan any time, any where, any how (David and Goliath). You cannot number, for example, how many people, nations and kingdoms that God destroyed to bring victory to the physical Israel! God is committed to your success.

You are His very seed. You are the apple of His eyes. Stop looking-down on yourself!

God is out against anybody that is against you, and He is against anything that is against you. Genesis 12:3, "I will bless them that bless thee, and curse him that curseth thee: and in thee shall all families of the earth be blessed." He will not allow you to be tossed around by anybody, group, government or authority.

You are a sensitive issue in God program. There is a touch not decree about you, based on the covenant.

Psalms 106:7-10, "Our fathers understood not thy wonders in Egypt; they remembered not the multitude of thy mercies; but provoked him at the sea, even at the Red sea. Nevertheless he saved them for his name sake, that he might make his mighty power to be known. He rebuked the Red sea also, and it was dried up: so he led them through the depths, as through the wilderness. And he saved them from the hand of him that hated them, and redeemed them from the hand of the enemy."

God will not tolerate your being messed-up or treated anyhow! No! It not part of the covenant. Those who attempted to wrong the people of Israel paid dearly for it. Those who attempted evil against Moses, even in the camp of Israel, paid for it. He will do anything to protect you, even if it means killing.

Zechariah 2:8–9, "For thus saith the LORD of hosts; After the glory hath he sent me unto the nations which spoiled you: for he that toucheth you toucheth the apple of his eye. For, behold, I will shake mine hand upon them, and they shall be a spoil to their servants: and ye shall know that the LORD of hosts hath sent me."

Nobody can take advantage of you and go free. Know that you are born of God.

"For whatsoever is born of God overcometh the world: and this is the victory that overcometh the world, even our faith." (1John 5:4).

God is interested in your winning always. If the physical Israel can win all their battles with impunity, you can do much more than that, because you're born of God.

The moment you got born again, you were translated from the earthly realm to the heavenly realm, where Satan is not permitted to win (Revelation 12:7–9). In that heavenly realm, you are a destined winner. You are not permitted to lose, you are not programmed to fail. Satan is not permitted to rear-up his head.

You can win always! The greater one is in you. He is at work in you now. He is greater than all your life battles. So you can stand in the face of any challenge, any assault of the devil and say to him: "Satan, get out!"

You are the righteousness of God

We are the Righteousness of God in Christ. 2Corinthians 5:21 "Him who knew no sin he made to be sin on our behalf; that we might become the righteousness of God in Christ."

Now He wants us to bear the fruit of Righteousness. 2Corinthians 9:10 "And increase the fruits of your righteousness."

Righteousness is the ability to stand in the Father's presence without condemnation. It gives us the legal right to the use of the name of Jesus. It gives us ability to stand in the presence of diseases of all kinds without fear, in the presence of Satan as an absolute master.

1John 2:29 "Everyone that doeth righteousness is begotten of God."

How few of us have ever done Righteousness. We have thought it meant only conduct, a carefulness in our walk. That is implied, but that is not "doing Righteousness."

Doing Righteousness is doing the works that Jesus accomplished, for we are taking His place. Righteousness gives us the ability to stand in the presence of God anytime and to stand in the presence of Satan as absolute victors.

How little this has been understood. How little we have majored it.

Now God is waiting for us to bring this truth to the front. e wants us to begin to live Righteousness, to practice Righteousness, to break Satan's dominion, to speak with authority just as Jesus did.

You have God's wisdom

You might say this is the summation of all.

If you have God's ability, God's wisdom, and you let them loose, what limitlessness there will be to your ministry. It is not a problem of education, but of letting God loose in you, liberating the ability of God that is within you.

Locked up in you today is the ability of God.

Jesus has been made wisdom unto you.

1Corinthians 1:30 "But of him are ye in Christ jesus, who was made unto us wisdom from God."

James told the babes in Christ that if they lacked wisdom they could ask for it of God. James 1:5-8 (Weymouth)

"And if any one of you is deficient in wisdom, let him ask God for it, who gives with open hand to all men, and without upbraiding; and it will be given him. But let him ask in faith and have no doubt; for he who has doubts is like the surge of the sea,"

You are complete in Him

Colossians 2:9–10, "for in him dwells the fullness of the Godhead bodily. And you are complete in him, which is the head of all principalities and powers".

In Christ, you cannot lack anything.

As for wisdom, the Bible says, "Christ has been made unto us wisdom" (1Corinthians 1:30).

As for health, the Bible says, "by his stripes we were healed" (1Peter 2:24).

As for wealth, the Bible says, "God shall supply all your need according to his riches in glory by Christ Jesus" (Philippians 4:19).

1John 3:2, "Beloved, now are we the sons of God, and it doth not yet appear what we shall be: but we know that, when he shall appear, we shall be like Him; for we shall see Him as he is."

Conclusion

The Christian is the one who is born of God, by confessing Jesus Christ as his Lord and saviour. This process of rebirth is what is called born again.

Exercise your faith by speaking the following with your mouth, and believing it in your heart:

1. I am a new being that have never existed before!

2. I belong to the family of God!

3. I have dominion over every circumstance!

4. I am seated in the place of power!

5. Greater is He that is in me, than he that is in the world!

6. By his stripes, I am healed!

7. As He is, so am I in this world!

8. I am the righteousness of God in Christ Jesus!

9. I can never be defeated! I am born to succeed! 10. I have God's wisdom!

11. I can do all things through Christ which strengthens

Chapter 3

HOW TO USE THE NAME OF JESUS

me!

12. I am complete in Him!

John 14:13–14 "And whatsoever ye shall ask in my name, that will I do, that the Father may be glorified in the Son. If ye shall ask any thing in my name, I will do it."

That word "Ask" means "Demand."

His Name is to be used in the sense that we see it used in Acts 3 by Peter who spoke to the impotent man at the gate of the temple saying, "In the name of Jesus Christ of Nazareth, Rise up and walk."

This is not prayer. This is casting out demons in that Name. There is healing for the sick in that Name. There is power to break disease and sickness in the hearts and lives of men in that Name.

That Name is yours. You may not have taken advantage of it. Jesus gave you the power of attorney to use His name. He said, "All authority hath been given unto me in heaven and on earth. Go ye therefore, and make disciples of all the nations." (Matthew 28:18–19).

The word "disciple" means student, one who learns. We are to make students of the Word of all nations.

You have the ability to go and do it. "In my name they shall cast out demons . . . they shall lay hands on the sick, and they shall recover." (Mark 16:17–18).

That belongs to you now. The age of miracles is your age. It is the present age.

You can live and walk in the fulness of God's ability. You can let that ability loose in you, if you will. This is love's challenge to let the life of God loose in you, to let the Word loose in you, to give the Name its real place in your life.

Can that Name of Jesus keep us from sickness? Can it keep us from want? Can it keep us from poverty, fear, and the dread of hunger and cold?

Can that Name be used just as Jesus suggested in Mark 16:18? "And these signs shall accompany them that believe: in my name shall they cast out demons; they shall speak with new tongues; they shall take up serpents, and if they drink any deadly thing, it shall in no wise hurt them; they shall lay hands on the sick, and they shall recover."

Peter understood this message, and in Acts 9:32–35: "And it

came to pass, as Peter passed throughout all quarters, he came down also to the saints which dwelt at Lydda. And there he found a certain man named Aeneas, which had kept his bed eight years, and was sick of the palsy. And Peter said unto him, Aeneas, Jesus Christ maketh thee whole: arise, and make thy bed. And he arose immediately. And all that dwelt at Lydda and Saron saw him, and turned to the Lord."

The early church was utterly independent of circumstances. I don't mean the whole church. I mean the apostles who understood fully the use of the Name of Jesus.

Men could be sick then by breaking fellowship and because of lack of knowledge, just as they can be today. The early church, that is the Gentile portion of it, had never had any Revelation from God. It was utterly raw material.

The Jews were in worse condition. They were Covenant breakers, as the modern church is.

The most difficult to deal with today are the most religious. If there was sickness in the early church, it was to be expected, because they had no precedent, no examples ahead of them.

Jesus came to destroy the works of the devil. We are His instruments to do His work. We are to destroy sickness in the church. Our new slogan is: "No more sickness in the body of Christ."

His Word is to become a reality in the lives of men. The fact that He bore our sins and put sin away by the sacrifice of

Himself, and that He made provision for the remission of all we have ever done or said, proves that we should not be sick or in bondage to sin.

He made the sacrifice for sins, the things we had done as a result of the sin nature.

The New Birth wipes out everything we have ever done.

2Corinthians 5:17, "Wherefore if any man is in Christ, he is a new creature: the old things are passed away; behold, they are become new."

Romans 8:1 becomes a reality. "There is therefore now no condemnation to them that are in Christ Jesus."

The people who are in Christ Jesus are sin free, disease free, condemnation free.

Let us then, arise, take our place, and go out and carry this message of deliverance and victory to others.

It is very important that we grasp clearly 1John 5:13, "These things have I written unto you, that ye may know that ye have eternal life, even unto you that believe on the name of the Son of God."

We have God's nature which gives us a perfect fellowship with the Father, a perfect right to use His Name, a perfect deliverance and freedom from Satan's dominion.

2Peter 1:4, "Whereby He hath granted unto us His precious and exceeding great promises; that through these ye may become partakers of the divine nature."

John 14:13–14, "And whatsoever ye shall ask in my name, that will I do, that the Father may be glorified in the Son. If ye shall ask any thing in my name, I will do it."

Romans 6:14, "For sin shall not have dominion over you: for ye are not under the law, but under grace."

If sin cannot have dominion over you, disease cannot have dominion over you, because they come from the same source.

The nature and life of God that has come into you will give you life and health.

Psalms 91:16, "With long life will I satisfy him, And show him my salvation."

We all admit that the ninety-first Psalm belongs to the church. It could not apply to the Jew, but it does apply to us.

"He will cover thee with His pinions, And under His wings shalt thou take refuge: His truth (or Word) is a shield and a buckler. Thou shalt not be afraid for the terror by night, Nor for the arrow that flieth by day; For the pestilence that walketh in darkness, Nor for the destruction that wasteth at noonday. A thousand shall fall at thy side, And ten thousand at thy right hand; But it shall not come nigh thee."

There is protection from earthquakes, from cyclones, pestilence, from sickness, from war.

NEW CREATION / 72

Chapter 4

YOUR RIGHTS IN CHRIST

This thing puts us into the realm of the supernatural. We are linked up with Christ so that He said, "I am the vine, ye are the branches: He that abideth in me, and I in him, the same bringeth forth much fruit: for without me ye can do nothing." (John 15:5).

This chapter addresses one of the very important areas of our Christian lives, our rights in Christ. The good understanding of this chapter is very important for every Christian because, like every area of life, if you don't know what belongs to you, you cannot enjoy them. Hosea 4:6, "My people perish for lack of knowledge".

Just like the woman whom the queen gave her whole estate to in her (queen's) will, continued living in penury (abject poverty), until a lawyer came to visit her and executed the will.

So this chapter teaches you of your entitlements.

You have Righteousness

Righteousness is the nature of God. It's the ability to stand in the presence of God without fear or any sense of inferiority or condemnation.

Righteousness is a free gift from God. You cannot earn it by working for it or by doing something to obtain it. It is a free gift made available to all through the substitutionary work of our Lord Jesus Christ. God's righteousness comes through faith in our Lord Jesus Christ.

You cannot grow or increase in righteousness, but you can grow in the consciousness of your righteousness. This helps the communication of your faith become effective and productive.

Philemon 6, "That the communication of thy faith may become effectual by the acknowledging of every good thing which is in you in Christ Jesus."

Righteousness is a gift. Romans 5:17, "For if by one man's offence death reigned by one; much more they which receive abundance of grace and of the gift of righteousness shall reign in life by one, Jesus Christ."

We are born of God and just as a dog gives birth to a dog with its nature and attributes, God gave birth to us with his nature (righteousness) and attributes (the fruit of the spirit). 2Corinthians 5:21, "For he hath made him to be sin for us, who knew no sin; that we might be made the righteousness of God in him."

There is an erroneous belief that righteousness is the

complete absence of sin but righteousness is not sinless. A man no matter how well he barks or walks on his two legs and hands cannot be called a dog. Likewise, no matter how well a monkey or a dog walks on their legs they cannot be called men.

Righteousness is not based on our ability not to transgress the law (not to sin). Galatians 2:21, "I do not frustrate the grace of God: for if righteousness come by the law, then Christ is dead in vain."

2Corinthians 5:21 says, "For He has made Him to be sin for us, who knew no sin, that we might be made the righteousness of God in Him".

Romans 10:1–4, "Brethren, my heart's desire and prayer to God for Israel is, that they might be saved. For I bear them record that they have a zeal of God, but not according to knowledge. For they being ignorant of God's righteousness, and going about to establish their own righteousness, have not submitted themselves unto the righteousness of God. For Christ is the end of the law for righteousness to every one that believeth."

2Corinthians 4:1, "Therefore seeing we have this ministry, as we have received mercy, we faint not."

You have Eternal Life

Animals, Trees and other living things each have their own kind of life. The life span of a chicken is different from that of a mortal man. The life span of tree is different from that of dog.

Now if we are sons of God we have the same quality of life: the indestructible life of God.

John 5:26, "For as the Father hath life in himself; so hath he given to the Son to have life in himself"

What is Eternal life? "God hath given to us eternal life, and this life is in his Son" (1John 5:11).

Is it possible for a man to live forever and not see death? Matthew 16:28, "Verily I say unto you, There be some standing here, which shall not taste of death, till they see the Son of man coming in his kingdom."

These are the questions we need to ponder on as we discuss Eternal life.

Eternal life is God's kind of life, an everlasting life, a life that cannot be cut short by anything like disease, sickness or death. John 5:24, "Verily, verily, I say unto you, He that heareth my word, and believeth on him that sent me, hath everlasting life, and shall not come into condemnation; but is passed from death unto life."

It is not acquired after a man is dead like some people think. John 3:16, "For God so loved the world, that he gave his only begotten Son, that whosoever believeth in him should not perish, but have everlasting life."

2Timothy 1:9–10, "Who hath saved us, and called us with an holy calling, not according to our works, but according to his own purpose and grace, which was given us in Christ

Jesus before the world began, But is now made manifest by the appearing of our Saviour Jesus Christ, who hath abolished death, and hath brought life and immortality to light through the gospel"

The Bible says in Romans 5:21, "That as sin hath reigned unto death even so grace reign through righteousness unto eternal life by Jesus Christ". Romans 6:23 says, "for the wages of sin is death but the gift of God is eternal life through Jesus Christ".

Eternal life is a gift of God. It is imparted into our spirit the moment we got born again.

God's love for man brought about the gift of eternal life and this life is in His Son Jesus. 1John 5:11–12,"And this is the record, that God hath given to us eternal life, and this life is in his Son. He that hath the Son hath life; and he that hath not the Son of God hath not life."

The Bible says (2Timothy 1:10) Jesus Christ abolished death and hath brought life and immortality to light, through the gospel. Immortality here means "eternal life" or "everlasting life". Legally, death has no hold on the new creation.

Death reigned over the fallen human race and the ordinary man had a life span of 70 years or at most 100 years. But the recreated human spirit has an everlasting life.

Jesus brought life and immortality to light through the gospel. He lets us know that in John 5:24, that he that hears HisWord and believes on Him that sent Him, hath everlasting life and shall not come into condemnation but is passed from death to life.

He says "*has* passed", *not* "*will* pass".

This lets us know that the moment we get born again we pass from death to life, an everlasting life, a life above sickness and death.

We do not work for it, just as a newborn baby does not work for its life. We inherited God's kind of life, because we are born of Him. *We are born of God.*

God is immortal, 1Timothy 1:17, "Now unto the King eternal, immortal, invisible, the only wise God, be honour and glory for ever and ever. Amen."

And Christ has brought life and immortality to us.

In Luke 4:18 Jesus said "The Spirit of the Lord is upon me, because he hath anointed me to preach the gospel to the poor; he hath sent me to heal the brokenhearted, to preach deliverance to the captives, and recovering of sight to the blind, to set at liberty them that are bruised".

The word Liberty has two meanings. In Luke 4:18, Liberty means to set free, to release.

In contrast to this, see Galatians 5:13, "For, brethren, ye have been called unto liberty; only use not liberty for an occasion to the flesh, but by love serve one another."

Also Galatians 2:4, "And that because of false brethren unawares brought in, who came in privily to spy out our liberty which we have in Christ Jesus, that they might bring us into bondage".

In these verses, Liberty means right, synonymous with authority, a legal right. We have freedom that empowers us with a legal right. Rights – a just claim, authority.

"Thou art no more a servant, but a son" (Galatians 4:7). A son has rights that the servants do not have.

The son has unlimited access to his father, but a servant does not. The servant might not have information concerning his master's business, but the son does.

These rights can be categorized into three: the right to choose, live, and rule.

You have the right to choose

The new creation is not a programmed robot; he has the Right to choose. "I call heaven and earth to record this day against you, that I have set before you life and death, blessing and cursing: therefore choose life, that both thou and thy seed may live" (Deuteronomy 30:19).

Christianity is not a religion were you loose your right to choose. You have the right to choose between life and death, but the unbeliever is subjected to death already, he has no right, he is under bondage.

Paul tells us of his dilemma on how he was caught between two options: to make a choice to die and be with Christ, or to live and fulfill the gospel. Philippians 1:21–25, "For to me to live is Christ, and to die is gain. But if I live in the flesh, this is the fruit of my labour: yet what I shall choose I wot not. For I am in a strait betwixt two, having a desire to depart, and to be with Christ; which is far better: Nevertheless to abide in the flesh is more needful for you. And having this confidence, I know that I shall abide and continue with you all for your furtherance and joy of faith"

In John 5:5–9, the Bible records that Jesus asked the man who had been lame for 38 years if he wanted to be healed. "Wilt thou be made whole?" (John 5:6).

Many instances have shown that many are ignorant of their rights in this life. Some say, 'maybe God put the sickness on me to make me humble', but that is absolutely wrong.

His will for us is to prosper, and be in good health even as our soul prospers. (3John 2), "Beloved, I wish above all things that thou mayest prosper and be in health, even as thy soul prospereth."

We have the right to choose.

You have the right to live

Because we have believed in Jesus Christ we have the right to live. The bible says whoever believes in him shall never die (Amplified Bible says shall never die at all).

This scripture in John 11:25–26 speaks of physical death: "Jesus said unto her, I am the resurrection, and the life: he that believeth in me, though he were dead, yet shall he live: And whosoever liveth and believeth in me shall never die.

Believest thou this?"

Yes many have quoted the scripture saying "And as it is appointed unto men once to die, but after this the judgment" (Hebrews 9:27). From this scripture, they say every human being must die, but we know that we have been crucified with "our Saviour Jesus Christ, who hath abolished death, and hath brought life and immortality to light through the gospel" (2Timothy 1:10).

Hebrews 11:5, "By faith Enoch was translated that he should not see death; and was not found, because God had translated him: for before his translation he had this testimony, that he pleased God."

Therefore the life, which we now live in the flesh, we live by faith of the Son of God.

Death is a choice. Romans 6:8–9, "Now if we be dead with Christ, we believe that we shall also live with him: Knowing that Christ being raised from the dead dieth no more; death hath no more dominion over him."

The Bible says death has no dominion over us. Death is a choice because Jesus abolished death and brought life and immortality.

The question that a lot of people ask is 'Why do some Christians still die?" The scriptures say in 1Corinthians 15:26, "The last enemy that shall be destroyed is death."

Death is still in existence. It has only been abolished but not yet destroyed.

Being abolished means it has no legal right upon us, but

except we lay down our lives, we have the right to live. A man could live without the sting of death, like Enoch and Elijah, who never died physically.

John 10:17–18, "Therefore doth my Father love me, because I lay down my life, that I might take it again. No man taketh it from me, but I lay it down of myself. I have power to lay it down, and I have power to take it again. This commandment have I received of my Father."

You have the right to rule

1Peter 2:9 says we are kings and priests, "ye are a chosen generation, a royal priesthood, an holy nation, a peculiar people; that ye should shew forth the praises of him who hath called you out of darkness into his marvellous light".

As kings, we have the right to rule. "Much more they which receive abundance of grace and of the gift of righteousness shall reign in life by one, Jesus Christ" (Romans 5:17). "Jesus Christ, who is . . . the prince of the kings of the earth" (Revelation 1:5).

To reign means to rule, to govern. We must walk with the mentality of a king, a peculiar people and a chosen generation. God has given us the divine ability to cause changes.

As kings our words are powerful when we speak, we speak word of power. "Where the word of a king is, there is power: and who may say unto him, What doest thou?" (Ecclesiastes 8:4).

The Bible says "Ye are gods; and all of you are children of the most High" (Psalms 82:6).

You have an inheritance in Christ

The new creation has an inheritance in Christ. Galatians 4:7 says, "wherefore thou art no more servants, but sons, and if sons, then heirs of God through Christ".

If heirs, then what is our inheritance? By the reason of Jesus's death, a will came into effect. "In whom also we have obtained an inheritance, being predestinated according to the purpose of him who worketh all things after the counsel of his own will" (Ephesians 1:11).

Our inheritance is our legal possession. No one can revoke the will that has been written about our inheritance. (Hebrews 9:15), "And for this cause he is the mediator of the new testament, that by means of death, for the redemption of the transgressions that were under the first testament, they which are called might receive the promise of eternal inheritance."

What are the things that are rightly yours? A man died in poverty because he did not know that his late father left him a huge inheritance.

What is our inheritance? Firstly, we must understand that according to scriptures we have obtained an inheritance. Colossians 1:12 says 'giving thanks unto the Father, which hath made us meet to be partakers of the inheritance of the saints in light" and 1Corinthians 3:21–23 tells us that *all things are yours*: "For all things are your's; Whether Paul, or Apollos, or Cephas, or the world, or life, or death, or things present, or things to come; all are your's; And ye are Christ's; and Christ is God's."

Everything your mind can receive is yours! Whether death, whether life, wealth, health, joy, houses, education; *all things are yours*.

Abraham received the promise as the heir of the world and the promise was also to his seed. Romans 4:13, "For the promise, that he should be the heir of the world, was not to Abraham, or to his seed, through the law, but through the righteousness of faith."

Psalms 115:16, "The heaven, even the heavens, are the Lord's: but the earth hath he given to the children of men."

Now our inheritance can be classified into general, which is all things, and then specifically into three, which are: divine health, prosperity and abundance, and deliverance.

As for divine health, God's will for us is to be in good health. In Isaiah 53:4–5, Surely he hath borne our griefs, and carried our sorrows: yet we did esteem him stricken, smitten of God, and afflicted. But he was wounded for our transgressions, he was bruised for our iniquities: the chastisement of our peace was upon him; and with his stripes we are healed" and 1Peter 2:24, God affirmed divine healing and divine health to us.

Isaiah 53:4–5 was a prophecy on health for the ordinary people. Verse 5 says "with his stripes we are healed". By the stripes of a man they had not yet seen, or known.

While divine healing is for the unsaved, divine Health is for the believer, 1Peter 2:24, "Who his own self bare our sins in his own body on the tree, that we, being dead to sins, should live unto righteousness: by whose stripes ye were healed."

For we being dead to sin should live unto righteousness, by whose stripes we were healed. It means: we have already been healed, because the scripture has been fulfilled!

Therefore, we have divine health as our inheritance. It is God's will for us to prosper and be in good health even as our souls prosper (3John 2).

Sin brings diseases, sickness and death. But we are the righteousness of God and sin has no dominion over us.

Health denotes freedom from sickness. It means fitness, well-being, wholeness.

As for Prosperity and Abundance, Someone said, 'I really don't want to be too rich'. But the Bible says God wants us to prosper and to have in abundance.

To prosper means to flourish. Poverty is a state of lack.

2Corinthians 8:9 says, Jesus became poor so that we through his poverty might become rich.

He has given us all things to enjoy. 1Timothy 6:17, "Charge them that are rich in this world, that they be not highminded, nor trust in uncertain riches, but in the living

God, who giveth us richly all things to enjoy"

God wants us to have in abundance so that we can be a blessing to others.

As for Deliverance, Colossians 1:12–13, "Giving thanks unto the Father, which hath made us meet to be partakers of the inheritance of the saints in light: Who hath delivered us from the power of darkness, and hath translated us into the kingdom of his dear Son"

God has delivered us and so it is wrong for a child of God to seek deliverance. Your body is the temple of the Holy Spirit.

The Bible says God has translated us into the kingdom of his Son. He has delivered us from the power of darkness, (The Amplified Bible, says ". . .and has drawn us to himself") and has translated us unto the kingdom of His dear Son.

Mark 16:17, "And these signs shall follow them that believe; In my name shall they cast out devils; they shall speak with new tongues"

We have the power to cast out demons, not for them to possess us.

You are God's address

An address is a place of residence. The new creation is God's house, His address.

Acts 17:24,25,28, "God that made the world and all things

therein, seeing that he is Lord of heaven and earth, dwelleth not in temples made with hands; Neither is worshipped with men's hands, as though he needed any thing, seeing he giveth to all life, and breath, and all things; . . . For in him we live, and move, and have our being; as certain also of your own poets have said, For we are also his offspring."

1Corinthians 6:19 lets us know that, He dwells in us, and that our body is the temple of the Holy Spirit. "What? know ye not that your body is the temple of the Holy Ghost which is in you, which ye have of God, and ye are not your own?"

Colossians 1:27 states "Christ in you, the hope of glory". New Living Translation puts it "Christ lives in you. This gives you assurance of sharing his glory." Amplified Bible says "guarantee of [realizing the] glory".

Ephesians 2:21–22, "In whom all the building fitly framed together groweth unto an holy temple in the Lord: In whom ye also are builded together for an habitation of God through the Spirit."

Jeremiah 51:20–22, "Thou art my battle axe and weapons of war: for with thee will I break in pieces the nations, and with thee will I destroy kingdoms; And with thee will I break in pieces the horse and his rider; and with thee will I break in pieces the chariot and his rider; With thee also will I break in pieces man and woman; and with thee will I break in pieces old and young; and with thee will I break in pieces the young man and the maid"

The Bible says we are God's extension, the extension of his manifested presence on earth. We execute justice, maintain peace through our prayers, and reshape situations.

Acts 1:8 says we shall receive power when the Holy Spirit comes upon us. That power is that dynamic ability to cause changes.

This honour has all the saints of God. Psalms 149:6–9, "Let the high praises of God be in their mouth, and a twoedged sword in their hand; To execute vengeance upon the heathen, and punishments upon the people; To bind their kings with chains, and their nobles with fetters of iron; To execute upon them the judgment written: this honour have all his saints. Praise ye the Lord."

"Ye are gods!"

This is a fundamental, powerful truth that, if for any reason it enters your heart, it will make you unshakable, immovable, triumphant, buoyant and blossoming! It will become a foundation that cannot be shaken! I've never seen a man come in contact with this and still be tossed about.

The enemy hates this. So he'll do anything to frustrate you from standing on such a revelation. But may the God of heaven, the great provider, provide you with such enlightenment in your heart, that will give you all of what this truth contains.

"I have said, *Ye are gods*; and all of you are children of the most High" (Psalms 82:6).

This is the dominion scripture of the saints. Get it once and live by it forever. This scripture was a turning point in my life. It came early enough in my Christian life, that I didn't have to be cheated for long.

There is an anointing upon the revelation of this scripture that is going to establish you in permanent authority over Satan. If you understand the mystery of this Psalms 82:6, you will be in complete charge over the affairs of life!

Ye are gods! This is the basis for the supernatural, that you are no longer human, you are superhuman, super, extra-natural. See yourself no more as an ordinary human being. That not the truth. The truth is that you are a son of God, so you are a god.

The son of a goat is a goat. The son of a man is a man. The son of God can't be anything else but a god, because in the law of creation, everything produces after its kind. That does not exempt God. Ye are gods!

Jesus re-echoed this statement in the New Testament, thus affirming its authenticity: "Jesus answered them, Is it not written in your law, I said, *Ye are gods*?" (John 10:34).

If you grasp this truth, every devil will see you and clear off the way! This is the fundamental secret of all my victories in life.

Others may call it blasphemy, but Jesus calls it "the scriptures". It is more profitable to believe the scriptures than all the gossips in the world.

If you don't want to fall like the princes, if you don't want to fail or be defeated like men, accept your peculiarity and walk in it forever, and for as long as you live, refuse to accept anymore that you are an ordinary human being.

Detest this lie from henceforth, and in every sphere of your life – your business, your career, ministry, family, etc. , accept the order of your divinity. Whatever is contained in God's divinity is yours to enjoy.

Let others experience whatsoever they like, your portion is only what the divinity of God carries – His peace, His joy, His wisdom, His life, His health, His strength, etc. In your family for example, you can enjoy the peace of God that passeth all understanding.

Life can indeed be dynamic, when you operate in the understanding of this unusual realm of the supernatural. Ye are gods! This is a vital truth that reveals your divinity. It places you in the very class of God.

With this truth in you, every devil will bow to you. Whatever God can break through, you too will break through. Whatever God can handle, you can handle.

You are just in the form of a man

Acts 3:22, "For Moses truly said unto the fathers, A prophet shall the Lord your God raise up unto you of your brethren, like unto me; him shall ye hear in all things whatsoever he shall say unto you."

When the Lord sent Moses to Pharaoh, He did not send him as a man. Exodus 7:1 says, "And the Lord said unto Moses, See, I have made thee a god to Pharaoh..."

Jesus came and was God unto the world. He came as God in the form of a man. And hear what Jesus said, "As my Father hath sent me, even so send I you" (John 20:21).

If you connect these two scriptures above, you will understand that you are only in the form of a man, you are not made of human stuff. There is something strange about your makeup!

The day you gave your life to Jesus, you received another life. You had human life before, now you have eternal life, which is the God-order of life. So you now operate the God-order of life within the form of an ordinary structure.

Carry the understanding therefore, that the same way Moses confronted Pharaoh, is the same way you are to handle Satan, in any way he presents himself.

It was not Moses that was able to get Israel out of Pharaoh hand, it was the greater one in him!

From now on, when the Pharaoh of this world (Satan) presents himself, look at him and pity him. Tell him, "Pharaoh, this is another Moses, the New Testament one. Now, get out, in Jesus name!"

Friend, another life has been infused and injected into you. It is eternal life – the very life of God! The Bible calls it "this treasure in earthen vessels" (2Corinthians 4:7).

An understanding of the image of God in us will translate us from the realm of human limitations, and put us right where things will work for us as they would for God.

If you don't have an understanding of the truth "Ye are gods", you will not be able to put situations on earth under control.

If you approach spiritual battles as a human being, you are bound to fail, because the flesh profiteth nothing. It is the spirit that quickeneth. By strength shall no man prevail.

Isaiah 59:19 says: "When the enemy shall come in like a flood, the Spirit of the Lord shall lift up a standard against him". Not a man height, status or the strength of his natural muscles, but the Spirit of God on the inside of him. This is the only way man can successfully put the enemy, Satan, where he belongs.

"I have said, Ye are gods; and all of you are children of the most High." Psalms 82:6

All of you that are the children of the Most High God are gods. And I mean all, not some, not a few. But because you don't know this, you are prone to die like men and fall like one of the princes.

You must know that by virtue of your new birth, you are no longer a mere being, but a peculiar being in human form. Everybody is free to be plagued by diseases, not you. Everybody is free to be frustrated in their various endeavors except you. The nobles of the earth may have no place to put their seats, not you.

I have said, "Ye are gods!"

You must understand in depth how this revelation is to affect your daily lifestyle. Besides, you must put it into practice. Ye are gods! Know it! Understand it! Walk in the reality of it! Work it out!

Be conscious of it

The knowledge of the Holy God, and the consciousness of His nature flowing in your veins, is your staff of office on the earth. Without it, you lose control.

You have the infallible nature of God that determines His own course and destiny, in your heart. You need to awaken your spiritual consciousness, and call off religion. We have been called to exhibit the transformed life on the earth. It time to show the devil that Jesus is still alive in us.

For your Pharaohs to submit to you, you must walk in the consciousness of the truth that says, "Ye are gods." For diseases to obey you, for sicknesses to bow to you, for poverty to give way to you, you must carry this consciousness about – that you are indeed a god in the form of a man.

Go and discover your roots, and live well!

From now on, every mountain will obey you. You were

once natural but now you are divine, because the life that makes for divinity now flows in you. Right now, whatever mountain you confront with this truth will obey you.

Get ready! Stop struggling! Start walking in the light of this revelation, and in no time at all, you will know that God who gives you dominion, backs it up with power.

You can dominate your circumstances! You can send sickness away from your house! You can send poverty away from your territory! You can have what you please, as long as it is covered by the covenant.

God's mirror principle

James 1:22–25, "But be ye doers of the word, and not hearers only, deceiving your own selves. For if any be a hearer of the word, and not a doer, he is like unto a man beholding his natural face in a glass: For he beholdeth himself, and goeth his way, and straightway forgetteth what manner of man he was. But whoso looketh into the perfect law of liberty, and continueth therein, he being not a forgetful hearer, but a doer of the work, this man shall be blessed in his deed."

A mirror is used to see ones image. It is a reflector; it shows the exact representation of the image before it.

The Bible lets us know that, God's word is His mirror and when we look into it we see our true reflection; whom God says we are. The mirror has the power to effect change in a person's life.

2 Corinthians 3:18 says, "But we all, with open face beholding as in a glass the glory of the Lord, are changed into the same image from glory to glory, even as by the Spirit of the Lord".

It does not matter how you feel or see yourself, it is what the mirror shows you that you are.

James 1:22–25 talks about being doers of the Word and not a forgetful hearer. It gives us a clear picture of a man who is not a doer of the word. The bible says such a person is like a man who beholds his natural face in a glass and straight away forgets what manner of man he was. A lot of Christians forget who they are because they do not dwell on the Word.

As we read the Word we become transformed, we become changed. We become more like Jesus. Romans 8:29 says He predestinated us "to be conformed to the image of His Son".

Note that the Word will do nothing until you act on it. The word reveals who we really are.

Operation of the five senses

The senses include hearing, seeing, talking, smelling, and feeling. They are in the physical perception, but the Lord wants us to live by faith.

Physical perception connotes carnality and the Bible says they that are carnal or in the flesh cannot please God (Romans 8:6–18). But the new creation is not in the flesh but in the Spirit. The Bible says in 2Corinthians 5:7 that, "we walk by faith and not by sight".

Hebrews 11:1 says "Now faith is the substance of things hoped for, the evidence of things not seen". We don't need to see to believe, because God Himself has said it. In John 20:29 Jesus says "Thomas, because thou hast seen me, thou hast believed: blessed are they that have not seen, and yet have believed."

2 Corinthians 4:18 says, "So we fix our eyes not on what is seen, but on what is unseen, since what is seen is

Chapter 5

THE PERSON OF
THE HOLY SPIRIT

temporary, but what is unseen is eternal".

Faith in Jesus Christ alone is all that we need to live the Christian life. You must develop or grow your faith by hearing the Word of God.

Conclusion

A Christian is the righteousness of God in Christ Jesus. He has eternal life, which is God's kind of life. He has the right to rule, to live and to choose. He has inheritance in Christ: all things, divine health, prosperity and abundance, and deliverance. He is the dwelling place of God.

The person of the Holy Spirit is vital to the existence of nthe Christian. It would have been impossible for Jesus to accomplish his earthly ministry without the Holy Spirit.

In fact, Jesus would not have been born without the Holy

Spirit. Today, What differentiates Christianity from all the religions of the world is the presence and power of the Holy Spirit, who resides in the church (the body of Christ).

A clear and proper understanding of the person of the Holy Spirit, His ministry in and through the Christian is vital if we must walk in all the fullness of the provision of our heavenly father. This study is designed to accomplish just that. But to do this we must first look at the Trinity.

Trinity depicts the Godhead that operates in three personalities yet one. According to 1John 5:7, "there are three that bear record in heaven, the father, the word and the Holy spirit and these three are one".

It is therefore important to note that in discussing the person of the Holy Spirit, we are invariably discussing the whole personality of the Godhead: God the father, the Son and the Holy Spirit.

Who is the Holy Spirit?

The Holy Spirit, which is the third person of the Godhead, is the Spirit of God and the Power of God. He is that Spirit that proceeds from the father and made manifest where the father pleases, and in the same wholeness of God as He is on the throne. The Holy Spirit is not in any way lesser than God the Father or God the Son. He is co-equal with God; He is Himself God in all of God's Omnipotence.

Until we begin to appreciate the Holy Spirit as a person and relate to him as such, we'll not be able to enjoy the full benefit of his presence. He is a person with a purpose to reveal to us the things that God has prepared for us that love Him, and that we might know the things that are freely given to us by God (1Corinthians 2:9,10,12).

How do we know that the Holy Spirit is a person? A person has a will, emotion and intellect: A will to determine or to take action, emotion to express feelings, and intellect to understand, apprehend and perceive. The Holy Spirit has all of these three.

His will is to dwell in us so that we could have the fullness of his benefits. The Holy Spirit has an unlimited reservoir of intelligence as evidenced in His revelation of hidden wisdom and through revelation of deep truths of God to us (1Corinthians 2:10). The Holy Spirit could be angry, grieved and blasphemed. He loves us with an everlasting love and has shed His love abroad in our heart (Romans 5:5).

John 14:16–20, "And I will pray the Father, and he shall give you **another Comforter**, that he may abide with you for ever; Even the Spirit of truth; whom the world cannot receive, because it seeth him not, neither knoweth him: but ye knowhim; for he dwelleth with you, and shall be in you. I will not leave you comfortless: I will come to you. Yet a little while, and the world seeth me no more; but ye see me: because I live, ye shall live also. At that day ye shall know that I am in my Father, and ye in me, and I in you."

The character of the Holy Spirit is properly described in the Greek words for "another Comforter": "Allos-

Parakletos'. The word 'Allos-Parakletos' has seven synonyms: Comforter, Counselor, Teacher, Helper, Strengthener, Intercessor and Standby.

He is the comforter

As a comforter, the Holy Spirit was sent primarily to comfort God's people. We (Christians) live in a world that is largely anti-God. God, knowing the opposition and persecution we would face as Christians, sent the Holy Spirit to us to be our source of comfort.

2 Corinthians 1:3, "Blessed be God, even the Father of our Lord Jesus Christ, the Father of mercies, and the God of all comfort"

The early disciples during the time of persecution walked in the fear of the Lord and in the comfort of the Holy Spirit; and they were greatly multiplied.

Acts 9:31, "Then had the churches rest throughout all Judaea and Galilee and Samaria, and were edified; and walking in the fear of the Lord, and in the comfort of the Holy Ghost, were multiplied."

He is the counselor

Isaiah 11:2, "And the spirit of the Lord shall rest upon him, the spirit of wisdom and understanding, the spirit of counsel and might, the spirit of knowledge and of the fear of the Lord"

Have you ever been faced with a moment of great decision? At such times you should turn to the Holy Spirit for guidance. The guidance of the Holy Spirit is available to every child of God.

We should all expect the Holy Spirit to be our guide. After all, "For as many as are led by the Spirit of God, they are the sons of God." (Romans 8:14).

Proverbs 20:27 says, "the spirit of a man is the candle of the Lord, searching all the inward parts of the belly". To live in continuous victory, we must be led by the Spirit of God.

He is the helper

Romans 8:26, "Likewise the Spirit also helpeth our infirmities: for we know not what we should pray for as we ought: but the Spirit itself maketh intercession for us with groanings which cannot be uttered."

Help – as defined by Oxford Advanced Learner's Dictionary – means "to make it easier for somebody to do something, to assist somebody." The Holy Spirit – as our helper – assists us to do all that God has called us to do. He makes it easy for us to live successfully as Christians in this corrupt world.

There are times when you are faced with a great task and you are wondering how you would succeed. Be sure of this, you are not walking alone.

For example, Higher Life is a ministry that God has marvelously helped. In just a short time of our starting, we have achieved so much. If it were not for the help of the Holy Spirit, we would not have achieved this much. We are conscious of this fact. That is why we know what we have done so far is just the beginning.

With His help, there is no telling what we can do and where we can go. Glory to God!

He is the strengthener

Philippians 4:13, "I can do all things through Christ which strengtheneth me."

God's Spirit gives strength to our inner man. Paul declared that He could do all things through Christ who strengthens him.

Isaiah 11:2 calls Him the Spirit of might, "And the spirit of the Lord shall rest upon him, the spirit of wisdom and understanding, the spirit of counsel and might, the spirit of knowledge and of the fear of the Lord;"

In the Old Testament, men like David, Samson, Elijah, etc., did mighty things by the power of the Spirit. In our days we can do much more.

I heard the story of a woman whose son got involved in a car accident, when she got to the car she single handedly lifted up the car and rescued the son. People who saw her were amazed afterwards, four strong men couldn't lift up that same car.

The Holy Spirit resident in our spirit is a source of great strength. If we stay full of Him, we can never experience defeat in our lives.

He is the intercessor

An intercessor is one who stands in the gap for another. According to Romans 8:26, we don't always know what to pray for as we ought. We can't possibly know in our natural mind everything we should pray about, in every situation and circumstance.

The Holy Spirit assists us in our prayers with groaning, which cannot be uttered in articulate speech.

He is the teacher

As a teacher, the Holy Spirit carried on the ministry of Jesus, which was to a large extent a teaching ministry.

1Corinthians 2:9–11, "But as it is written, Eye hath not seen, nor ear heard, neither have entered into the heart of man, the things which God hath prepared for them that love him. But God hath revealed them unto us by his Spirit: for the Spirit searcheth all things, yea, the deep things of God. For what man knoweth the things of a man, save the spirit of man which is in him? Even so the things of God knoweth no man, but the Spirit of God."

When we receive the Holy Spirit, He indwells our spirit

man; He serves as a teacher to our spirit.

1 John 2:20, "But ye have an unction from the Holy One, and ye know all things."

We must realize that the things of God cannot be understood by the natural mind, but they are revealed to our spirits; it is with our spirit that we contact God.

John 16:13, "Howbeit when he, the Spirit of truth, is come, he will guide you into all truth: for he shall not speak of himself; but whatsoever he shall hear, that shall he speak: and he will shew you things to come."

As a teacher, He reveals to us the hidden mysteries of the kingdom of God. Non-Christians cannot understand why we do the things we do. But we have unction from the Holy one and we know all things (1John 2:20). As our teacher, He also reveals to us things to come (John 16:13).

We must realize that the Holy Spirit is in us to teach us all things. Most times, when I want to study God's Word I pray this simple prayer, "O blessed Holy Spirit, unveil the truth unto my spirit that I may stand in the fullness of the provision of my father, for He is my father, I love Him and He loves me".

He has made studying God's word a joyful experience for me.

He is the standby

Anytime we are in church during a service and there is an

interruption in power supply, we always put on our standby generator. The Holy Spirit is also referred to as the standby.

In John 14:17, Jesus said the Holy Spirit shall be in us and with us, "Even the Spirit of truth; whom the world cannot receive, because it seeth him not, neither knoweth him: but ye know him; for he dwelleth with you, and shall be in you."

Paul went through different experiences that revealed certain weaknesses in His life. The good thing was that even in the midst of his weakness, the Holy Spirit was at hand to strengthen him.

2 Corinthians 12:9–10, "But as it is written, Eye hath not seen, nor ear heard, neither have entered into the heart of man, the things which God hath prepared for them that love him. But God hath revealed them unto us by his Spirit: for the Spirit searcheth all things, yea, the deep things of God. For what man knoweth the things of a man, save the spirit of man which is in him? Even so the things of God knoweth no man, but the Spirit of God."

We can also enjoy this ministry of the Holy Spirit in our lives.

There are times when we are overwhelmed by issues and circumstances that reveal weaknesses in us. At such times we should remember the Holy Spirit as our standby.

God has promised that He would never leave us nor forsake us, Hebrews 13:5, "for he hath said, I will never leave thee, nor forsake thee."

Every Christian can receive the Holy Spirit

The scriptures let us know that the Spirit has been poured out on all flesh.

Joel 2:28, "And it shall come to pass afterward, that I will pour out my spirit upon all flesh; and your sons and your daughters shall prophesy, your old men shall dream dreams, your young men shall see visions"

Acts 2:17, "And it shall come to pass in the last days, saith God, I will pour out of my Spirit upon all flesh: and your sons and your daughters shall prophesy, and your young men shall see visions, and your old men shall dream dreams"

This means the Holy Spirit has been made available for all to receive. Acts 2:38–39, "Then Peter said unto them, Repent, and be baptized every one of you in the name of Jesus Christ for the remission of sins, and ye shall receive the gift of the Holy Ghost. For the promise is unto you, and to your children, and to all that are afar off, even as many as the Lord our God shall call."

The only requirement for receiving the Holy Spirit is for one to be born again. Luke 11:13, "If ye then, being evil, know how to give good gifts unto your children: how much more shall your heavenly Father give the Holy Spirit to them that ask him?"

The Holy Spirit responds to hunger and fills those

Christians who desire Him. Isaiah 44:3, "For I will pour water upon him that is thirsty, and floods upon the dry ground: I will pour my spirit upon thy seed, and my blessing upon thine offspring"

Fellowship with the Spirit

Fellowship is explained in the Chamber's English Dictionary as "Companionship". The dictionary further calls it a "Laying together".

It is a relationship, a process that circles around two or more individuals. It is an affair;

Fellowship with the Holy Spirit is a love affair between the Spirit of God and us.

The word fellowship is best described by the Greek word 'Koinonia'. Koinonia is an all round word for fellowship, which gives a further insight with three words: Communication, Communion and Transportation.

Communication is simply the transference of information between two or more individuals with feedback. In our fellowship with the Holy Spirit, we are engaged in communication with Him. A communication that comes about as a result of our relationship with him.

We speak to Him knowing that the he will surely answer, 1John 5:14–15, "And this is the confidence that we have in him, that, if we ask any thing according to his will, he heareth us: And if we know that he hear us, whatsoever we ask, we know that we have the petitions that we desired of him."

Communion is oneness, togetherness, a binding, a gluing, and identification. Communion with the Holy Spirit tells us who we are, and that we are one with Him, "For by one spirit are we all baptized into one body and have all been made to drink into one spirit" (1 Corinthians 12:13).

Transportation is the conveyance (movement) of goods and people from one place to another. You may ask how does this concern the Christian and his relationship with the Holy Spirit? There are times when you fellowship with the Holy Spirit and He will carry you (John 16:13).

The Holy Spirit makes the difference in the Christian's life.

The life of the Christian should be different, and this can be made possible only by the in filling of the Holy Spirit. In John 16:12–13, Jesus Himself said, "I have yet many things to say to you, but ye cannot bear them now. Howbeit when He, the Spirit of truth, is come, He will guide you into all truth..."

The unbeliever does not know the things to come, but the Holy Spirit reveals this to the Christian. The Christian is the man that has hope in this world.

The Holy Spirit makes the life of the Christian fruitful. Without Him, the life of the Christian is like a flower that does not receive daily nutrient.

Isaiah 32:15, "Until the spirit be poured upon us from on

high, and the wilderness be a fruitful field, and the fruitful field be counted for a forest."

This is the difference between the Spirit filled Christian and the Christian that is not filled with the Holy Spirit.

With the in filling of the Holy Spirit, any dryness in the Christian turns to fruitfulness and fruitfulness to abundance (forest). The person of the Holy Spirit is Christ in you, the hope of glory (Colossians 1:27).

His ministry through Christians

It is only by the power of the Holy Spirit that we can be effective witnesses of the death, burial and resurrection of our Lord Jesus Christ.

Jesus Christ said to his disciples that they would receive power after the Holy Spirit is come upon them (Acts 1:8).

This power is to enable them fulfill the ministry that he has called them into.

All Christians have been called into this ministry, "For the perfecting of the saints, for the work of the ministry, for the edifying of the body of Christ: Till we all come in the unity of the faith, and of the knowledge of the Son of God, unto a perfect man, unto the measure of the stature of the fulness of Christ" (Ephesians 4:12–13).

Luke 4:17–18 records our function or responsibilities in this ministry, "And there was delivered unto him the book of the prophet Esaias. And when he had opened the book, he found the place where it was written, The Spirit of the Lord is upon me, because he hath anointed me to preach the gospel to the poor; he hath sent me to heal the brokenhearted, to preach deliverance to the captives, and recovering of sight to the blind, to set at liberty them that are bruised"

Chapter 6

THE IMPORTANCE OF THE HOLY SPIRIT IN A CHRISTIAN'S LIFE

The Holy Spirit empowers all Christians to do the following: Preach the gospel to the poor, Heal the broken hearted, Preach deliverance to the captives, Recover the sight of the blind, and Set at liberty them that are bruised.

Conclusion

The Holy Spirit is the third person of the Godhead. He helps the Christians to live victorious lives, through His character: comforter, counselor, teacher, helper, strengthener, intercessor and standby.

It is very vital for a Christian to be intimately related to Him, by constantly fellows hipping with Him.

The importance of the Holy Spirit in the life of a believer can never be over emphasized.

The Holy Spirit is the gift of God to everyone who believes,

Acts 10:45, "And they of the circumcision which believed were astonished, as many as came with Peter, because that on the Gentiles also was poured out the gift of the Holy Ghost."

Hebrews 2:4, Amplified Bible, "[and besides this evidence] God also testifying with them [confirming the message of salvation], both by signs and wonders and by various miracles [carried out by Jesus and the apostles] and by [granting to believers the] gifts of the Holy Spirit according to His own will."

The earthly ministry of Jesus started after he had received the Holy Spirit.

In several instances, such as in Luke 24:49, he told His disciples to remain in Jerusalem till they have received the Holy Spirit and in Acts 1:8, He says, "And you shall receive power after the Holy Ghost is come upon you..."

This power refers to the dynamic ability to reproduce itself and it brings efficiency and might into the life of the believer as the very presence of God is brought to the believer.

A sign of being filled with God's Spirit is by speaking in other tongues, Mark 16:17, "And these signs shall follow them that believe; In my name shall they cast out devils; they shall speak with new tongues".

Acts 19:6, "And when Paul had laid his hands upon them, the Holy Ghost came on them; and they spake with tongues, and prophesied."

Speaking in tongues and its purposes

Speaking in tongues is an outpouring of divine communication from our inner most being to God; thereby cutting off the opportunity for the wicked one's comprehension.

1Corinthians 14:2, "For he that speaketh in an unknown tongue speaketh not unto men, but unto God: for no man understandeth him; howbe it in the spirit he speaketh mysteries."

You speakmysteries to God, a language of the Spirit that only God understands.

The main purposes are the following: To edify yourself, To build up your faith, To glorify God, To speak mysteries to God, and because it is a sign of the believer.

When we speak in tongues we edify ourselves, improve and strengthen ourselves. 1Corinthians 14:4, "He that speaketh in an unknown tongue edifieth himself; but he that prophesieth edifieth the church." As we speak in other tongues we build up our faith. Jude 20, "But ye, beloved, building up yourselves on your most holy faith, praying in the Holy Ghost."

Each believer has been given a measure of faith. This measure can be improved upon through prayer.

Speaking in other tongues is an effective way of praying to God because at that time it is your spirit that prays (1Corinthians 14:4). Boldness comes to your Spirit as you speak in other tongues.

Acts 10:46, "For they heard them speak with tongues, and magnify God."

There is a great depth at which you will worship God when you have the in filling of the Holy Spirit and worship Him in other tongues. Your mind is no more at work here but you worship Him in spirit and in truth, John 4:23, "But the hour cometh, and now is, when the true worshippers shall worship the Father in spirit and in truth: for the Father seeketh such to worship him."

God is a Spirit and we must relate to Him that way.

1Corinthians 14:2, "For he that speaketh in an unknown tongue speaketh not unto men, but unto God: for no man understandeth him; howbeit in the spirit he speaketh mysteries."

Because of the unfruitfulness of the mind (1Corinthians 14:14) you speak secret truths and hidden things not obvious to the understanding yet. This means you speak mysteries unto God.

This leads you to receiving divine revelations as you speak them.

Jesus said it emphatically that speaking in tongue is a sign of knowing those who have believed, "And these signs shall follow them that believe; In my name shall they cast out devils; they shall speak with new tongues" (Mark 16:17).

The difference between Mark 16:17 and 1Corinthians 12:10 is that in Mark 16:17, the signs of the believer is seen and speaking in tongues is a sign that must follow all who believe, while in 1Corinthians 12:10, we see the gifts of the Holy Spirit enumerated. "The Holy Spirit to each individual distributes these gifts as He wills" (1Corinthians 12:11).

These gifts are distributed differently to every individual according to God's own will (Hebrews 2:4).

The gifts of the Holy Spirit

1Corinthians 12:6–11, "And there are diversities of operations, but it is the same God which worketh all in all. But the manifestation of the Spirit is given to every man to profit withal. For to one is given by the Spirit the *word of wisdom*; to another the *word of knowledge* by the same Spirit; To another *faith* by the same Spirit; to another the *gifts of healing* by the same Spirit; To another the working of *miracles*; to another *prophecy*; to another *discerning of spirits*; to another *divers kinds of tongues*; to another the *interpretation of tongues*: But all these worketh that one and the selfsame Spirit, dividing to every man severally as he will."

These gifts are nine in number and they bear testimony of the truth of God's Word and God's calling upon a man's life. They are like equipment God has given to us for our work as believers.

They can further be classified into 3 categories: Power gifts, Utterance or vocal gifts and Revelation or inspirational gifts.

Power gifts are action gifts that cause someone to do or accomplish something and they include: Gift of healing, Faith and Working of miracles.

Utterance or vocal gifts make use of the vocals and they include: Prophecy, Interpretation of tongues and Speaking in diverse kinds of tongues.

Revelation or inspirational gifts make one to know or see a truth about another or about a situation. These are: Word of wisdom, Word of knowledge and discerning of Spirits (supernatural insights into the realm of spirits).

These gifts of the Spirit are what God uses to equip the ministry.

Ministry gifts

Ephesians 4:7–8, "But unto every one of us is given grace according to the measure of the gift of Christ. Wherefore he saith, When he ascended up on high, he led captivity captive, and gave gifts unto men."

These gifts are called the *five-fold ministry gifts* and they are: Prophets, Pastors, Evangelists, Teachers and Apostles, as seen in Ephesians 4:10–11.

Ephesians 4:10–13, "And he gave some, *apostles*; and some, *prophets*; and some, *evangelists*; and some, *pastors* and *teachers*; For the perfecting of the saints, for the work of the ministry, for the edifying of the body of Christ: Till we all come in the unity of the faith, and of the knowledge of the Son of God, unto a perfect man, unto the measure of the stature of the fulness of Christ"

God gives the Ministry gifts to individuals for the work of the ministry (Ephesians 4:12). These gifts have been given to the body of Christ by God to bring a balance in Church. This balance is vitally important for effectiveness.

The ultimate goals of all ministry gifts are for: The perfecting of the saints, Edifying the body of Christ, Unifying men in faith and knowledge, Perfecting the Church in Christ and Bringing men to maturity in Christ. All these goals can be seen in Ephesians 4:12–13.

Apostle

The word Apostle comes from the Greek word 'apostolos'. Translated, it means 'sent forth' or 'sent one'. An postle is one with a commission. It could be to establish churches, 1Corinthians 9:2, "If I be not an apostle unto others, yet doubtless I am to you: for the seal of mine apostleship are ye in the Lord." and 1Corinthians 4:15, "For though ye have ten thousand instructers in Christ, yet have ye not many fathers: for in Christ Jesus I have begotten you through the gospel."

An Apostle is first and foremost a preacher or a teacher of

the word, 1Timothy 2:7, "Whereunto I am ordained a preacher, and an apostle, (I speak the truth in Christ, and lie not;) a teacher of the Gentiles in faith and verity." and 2Timothy 1:11, "Whereunto I am appointed a preacher, and an apostle, and a teacher of the Gentiles."

An Apostle is sent forth with a particular message. His distinguished result is the ability to establish churches, as he may have to oversee the churches until they have been fully established (1Corinthians 9:1–2).

This office seems to embrace all other ministry gifts, as the apostle will do the work of the Teacher and a Pastor. As a teacher, he will teach and establish people. As a pastor he will pastor and shepherd the people for a while.

Prophet

The Prophet Speaks from the impulse of a sudden inspiration, from the light of a sudden revelation at that moment. He speaks by direct divine inspiration, an immediate revelation. He is also first of all a preacher or a teacher of the Word.

Evangelist

An Evangelist is one who brings the Evangel (the Good News); a messenger of good tidings. He brings the news of the redeeming grace of God and his favourite theme is salvation in its simplest form. He has a divine urge or burning within to preach the Word and get people saved.

Pastor

The word Pastor is Latin and means Shepherd. He is a Shepherd of God's Sheep in the local body and they are necessary for maturing, nurturing and equipping of the Saints.

Teacher

This is a divine gift and is about the calling placed on particular individuals to stand in that office and teach by supernatural abilities. It is a divine endowment to teach God's word.

Difference between the gifts of the Holy Spirit and ministry gifts

The Ministry gifts are God's calling into an office and cannot be desired, Hebrews 5:4, "And no man taketh this honour unto himself, but he that is called of God, as was Aaron."

It is God Himself who calls the individual into the fivefold ministry, (Ephesians 4:11), and no man can take it upon himself.

The ministry into which one is called is not in name but in power; for even if one calls himself into an office, it doesn't make him what he calls himself. The ministry must be evident in the individual's life because God who has called him will surely equip him with the divine enablement or endowment to stand in that office.

On the other hand Spiritual gifts can be desired, 1Corinthians 12:31, "But covet earnestly the best gifts: and yet shew I unto you a more excellent way."

Romans 1:11, "For I long to see you, that I may impart unto you some spiritual gift, to the end ye may be established;"

Though it is the Holy Spirit who gives out as He wills or chooses, "that one and the selfsame Spirit, dividing to every man severally as he will" (1Corinthians 12:11).

Differences between the gifts of the Holy Spirit and fruit of the recreated human spirit

The gifts of the Spirit are by impartation into man's spirit and they are abilities God gives to every believer to fulfill God's call upon his life.

The fruit of the spirit are nine in number (Galatians 5:23) and they are the fruit a believer is supposed to produce by reason of the Holy Spirit dwelling in him.

The believer has a level of control over the development of these fruit in his life. That is why Paul says, "If we live in the Spirit, let us also walk in the Spirit" (Galatians 5:25) and those who belong to Christ have crucified the flesh with its passion, appetites and desires. (Galatians 5:24).

The believer has the responsibility of ensuring that he bears the right fruit.

Every Christian can walk in the power of the Holy Spirit

The Holy Spirit has been given to us as was promised by God through Jesus Christ. It is left for every believer to receive him for he has already been made available for us all. All an individual needs to do is to desire him in all of his fullness.

Psalms 63:1–3,8, "O God, thou art my God; early will I seek thee: my soul thirsteth for thee, my flesh longeth for thee in a dry and thirsty land, where no water is; To see thy power and thy glory, so as I have seen thee in the sanctuary. Because thy lovingkindness is better than life, my lips shall praise thee. . . .My soul followeth hard after thee: thy right hand upholdeth me."

The Psalmist here has a deep hunger and desire for the presence of God – i.e. the Holy Spirit, who is also called the angel of God's presence, Isaiah 63:9–10, "In all their affliction He was afflicted, and the angel of His presence saved them: in His love and in His pity He redeemed them; and He bare them, and carried them all the days of old. But they rebelled, and vexed His holy Spirit: therefore He was turned to be their enemy, and He fought against them."

Desire and hunger and you will be filled, for Jesus says in

Matthew 5:6, "Blessed are they which do hunger and thirst after righteousness: for they shall be filled."

Even in having the desire you are blessed and you will be filled. The most important thing is the desire of the Holy Spirit. For all that believe or desire shall receive.

In the case of the apostles as we see in the scriptures, a desire had been placed in their hearts long before they received, John 14:16–17, "And I will pray the Father, and He shall give you another Comforter, that He may abide with you for ever; Even the Spirit of truth; whom the world cannot receive, because it seeth him not, neither knoweth him: but ye know him; for he dwelleth with you, and shall be in you." and in Acts 1:8, "But ye shall receive power, after that the Holy Ghost is come upon you: and ye shall be witnesses unto me both in Jerusalem, and in all Judaea, and in Samaria, and unto the uttermost part of the earth."

We see where Jesus told them to tarry in Jerusalem till they had been endued with power from on high, Luke 24:49, "And, behold, I send the promise of my Father upon you: but tarry ye in the city of Jerusalem, until ye be endued with power from on high." (repeated in Acts 1:4).

There was great anticipation and hunger in them and they were actually in the temple praying and expecting Him until He came as we see in Acts 2. This was important for them to have the ability to effectively minister the Word of God and live the Christian life.

In Isaiah 32:15, we see what happens to a man's life when God's Spirit is poured forth into him. "Until the spirit be poured upon us from on high, and the wilderness be a fruitful field, and the fruitful field be counted for a forest." It brings productivity and fruitfulness. The Spirit changes things and causes you to increase greatly.

In Isaiah 44:2–4, God speaks again about desire saying, "... I will pour water upon him that is thirsty and floods upon the dry ground: I will pour my Spirit upon thy seed and my blessing upon thine offspring: and they shall spring up as among the grass, as willows by the water courses."

Jesus says in John 7:37–38 that, "if any man thirsts, let him come to me and drink."

Note

It is however important to note that there is a difference between the in filling of the Holy Spirit, and the baptism of the Holy Ghost.

The word baptism is taken from the Greek word "baptizo", which means to be immersed or dipped into. This actually took place the day we got born again, for we were immersed into the body of Christ by the Holy Spirit.

The in filling however means you are filled with God's Spirit and given supernatural strength as a believer. The Spirit of God fills the believer to enable him be an effective

Chapter 7

THE CHURCH OF CHRIST

witness of Christ, Acts 2:4, "And they were all filled with the Holy Ghost, and began to speak with other tongues, as the Spirit gave them utterance."

Conclusion

This chapter emphasized the importance of the Holy Spirit to the life of Christian.

A lot of emphasis was laid on speaking in tongues, which is one of the Nine gifts of the Holy spirit to the Christian. This is because it is the gift that a Christian can use to build himself up. Jude 20; 1Corinthians 14:2.

This chapter also differentiated the five ministry gifts which are: *Apostle, Prophet, Evangelist, Pastor and Teacher*, from the nine gifts of the Holy Spirit.

Lastly, we learned that every Christian can work in the power of the Holy Spirit.

The Church has been God's plan from the beginning to establish His kingdom here on earth. In the Old Testament, God set the children of Israel free from the land of Egypt for them to worship Him. This is the first time we heard about the "Church in the wilderness". That is, God called the children of Israel out of Egypt, which gives the actual meaning of the Church "the called out ones"

What is the universal Church and how do I become a member?

Many people do not really understand what the word Church means. They talk about the "Protestant" Church or the "Catholic" or "Baptist" Church, while others actually think the Church is the building in which Christians meet.

The Greek word translated Church is ECCLESIA, which means a gathering of people called out from among other people. The New Testament describes the word Church in two ways.

On the one hand, it is used for all believers on earth. This is the Church, which is called Christ's body, Colossians 1:18,24, "And he is the head of the body, the church ... For his body's sake, which is the church" and 1Corinthians 12:12–13,27, "For as the body is one, and hath many members,..."

On the other hand, the word Church is used to refer to all believers in the local Church, 1Corinthians 16:19, "The churches of Asia salute you. Aquila and Priscilla salute you much in the Lord, with the church that is in their house."

One becomes a member of the Church by believing in one's heart that Jesus Christ died on the cross of Calvary for one and confessing with one's mouth that Jesus is one's Lord and personal saviour, Romans 10:9–10, "That if thou shalt confess with thy mouth the Lord Jesus, and shalt believe in thine heart that God hath raised him from the dead, thou shalt be saved. For with the heart man believeth unto righteousness; and with the mouth confession is made unto salvation."

The purpose of the Church and its local assemblies

The purpose of the Church is to Glorify God and to witness to the world. The true purpose of the Church is to be a light, (Isaiah 60:1), "Arise, shine; for thy light is come, and the glory of the Lord is risen upon thee." and to glorify God in all our works and deeds, mindful of the fact that He is the Lord of our lives, our source and strength Ephesians 3:21, "Unto him be glory in the church by Christ Jesus throughout all ages, world without end. Amen."

The aim of the Church is to bear witness of Christ to sinners. We are to tell the world about the Lord Jesus and the work He did on the cross of Calvary so that all men might be saved. Therefore the local assembly should witness to the people in the place where it is located, Matthew 18:20, "For where two or three are gathered together in my name, there am I in the midst of them." The local assembly should also send forth Christians to take the message of salvation to people in other lands Mark 16:15–18, "And he said unto them, Go ye into all the world, and preach the gospel to every creature. He that believeth and is baptized shall be saved; but he that believeth not shall be damned. And these signs shall follow them that believe; In my name shall they cast out devils; they shall speak with new tongues; They shall take up serpents; and if they drink any deadly thing, it shall not hurt them; they shall lay hands on the sick, and they shall recover."

The local assembly actually is a gathering of believers in a given locality. We need local assemblies in order to bear witness of Christ. The gold lamp stands in Revelation 1:20 as a picture of a local assembly and gold speaks of divine righteousness. "The mystery of the seven stars which thou sawest in my right hand, and the seven golden candlesticks. The seven stars are the angels of the seven churches: and the seven candlesticks which thou sawest are the seven churches."

The local assembly positions the individual believer in the body of Christ and enables him or her function properly, 1Corinthians 12:26, "And whether one member suffer, all the members suffer with it; or one member be honoured, all the members rejoice with it."

The local assembly also builds up the individual member, thereby nourishing him or her onto maturity. The local assembly also enables the believer discover the different gifts bestowed on him by the Holy Spirit.

"Upon this rock I'll build my church" — is the rock Peter?

No, the rock is not Peter. In Greek, the name Peter is Petros (small rock), while rock is Petra.

Jesus Christ said in Matthew 16:18, "you are Peter (Petros) and upon this rock (Petra) I'll build my church." In this verse of scripture he was first talking about the revelation of the person of Jesus. He meant that the Church is built out of those stones (small rock) that partake of the nature of the Petra (rock) by their confession of him.

Peter's answer as to who Jesus is, sets apart from and beyond human reasoning as Jesus commended his having heard from God, Matthew 16:16–17, "And Simon Peter answered and said, Thou art the Christ, the Son of the living God. And Jesus answered and said unto him, Blessed art thou, Simon Barjona: for flesh and blood hath not revealed it unto thee, but my Father which is in heaven."

Afterward, Jesus emphasized that leadership in His church would always be based not on man's ability to reason things out, but on his readiness and receptivity to hear God through revelation knowledge.

So Christ is actually the chief cornerstone and the firm foundation upon which every Christian's faith is built. 1Peter 2:4–7, "To whom coming, as unto a living stone, disallowed indeed of men, but chosen of God, and precious, Ye also, as lively stones, are built up a spiritual house, an holy priesthood, to offer up spiritual sacrifices, acceptable to God by Jesus Christ. Wherefore also it is contained in the scripture, Behold, I lay in Sion a chief corner stone, elect, precious: and he that believeth on him shall not be confounded. Unto you therefore which believe he is precious: but unto them which be disobedient, the stone which the builders disallowed, the same is made the head of the corner,"

Ephesians 2:18–20, "For through him we both have access by one Spirit unto the Father. Now therefore ye are no more strangers and foreigners, but fellow citizens with the saints, and of the household of God; And are built upon the foundation of the apostles and prophets, Jesus Christ himself being the chief corner stone".

1Corinthians 3:11, "For other foundation can no man lay than that is laid, which is Jesus Christ."

Is it important to belong to a church?

It is important to belong to a Church because the Bible says we should not neglect the coming together of God's people as in fellowship, Hebrews 10:25, "Not forsaking the assembling of ourselves together, as the manner of some is; but exhorting one another: and so much the more, as ye see the day approaching."

We also belong to a Church so as to grow spiritually onto maturity.

Also, it makes us consistent and committed members of the body of Christ (Ephesians 4:11–14).

Who builds the church

Jesus is the builder, Matthew 16:18, "And I say also unto thee, That thou art Peter, and upon this rock I will build my church; and the gates of hell shall not prevail against it."

He is the rock of ages in whom there is salvation.

Jesus Christ is the true foundation of the Christian's life, 1Peter 2:6, "Wherefore also it is contained in the scripture, Behold, I lay in Sion a chief corner stone, elect, precious: and he that believeth on him shall not be confounded."

He started building when He died on the cross of Calvary for all men.

We are also builders.

We are builders also because when we believed, we began to exist as members of the body of Christ and therefore we need to take our place in the body of Christ Ephesians 4:12, "for the edifying of the body of Christ" and "for the perfecting of the saints".

We are co-labourers.

We are partners with deity, because God has chosen us as co-laborers in his vineyard and therefore we are God's husbandry and his building, 1Corinthians 3:9–10, "For we are labourers together with God: ye are God's husbandry, ye are God's building. According to the grace of God which is given unto me, as a wise master builder, I have laid the foundation, and another buildeth thereon. But let every man take heed how he buildeth thereupon."

We are in partnership with God and we have been given the ministry of reconciliation whereby we reconcile souls back to him.

Why should I go to Church?

To function as a member of the body of Christ (1Corinthians 12:12–26)

To build ourselves up in the most holy faith (Jude 20).

To serve, which is in coming together as members of the body of Christ, the Holy Spirit helps each believer to worship God and witness Christ.

(Ephesians 4:11–14; Hebrews 10:25)we go to Church so that we can build others and to be built up to maturity.

The Great Exchange

Conclusion

The Church of Jesus Christ is the body of all believers. One becomes part of the Church by being born again.

The Church's primary purpose is to glorify God and witness Christ to the world. It is required of every Christian to identify with a local assembly and fellowship with them. Participating in fellowship is not optional. Hebrews 10:25 admonishes us not to forsake the assembly of the brethren, "Not forsaking the assembling of ourselves together, as the manner of some is; but exhorting one another: and so much the more, as ye see the day approaching."

Lastly, a Christian is a co-labourer with God in building the Church.

2 Corinthians 5:21, "For He made Him who knew no sin to be sin for us, that we might become the righteousness of God in Him."

Is it boasting to say that we are 100 percent righteous? Not at all!

But by speaking what the Gospel says and confessing what God says, not of our own works!

This brings us to the question: How are we then 100 percent righteous?

First, we shall take a closer look at how we became sinners.

The Bible tells us that by one man's disobedience (Adam's), we all became sinners, and by one man's obedience (Jesus Christ) we obtain Righteousness. Romans 5:19, "For as by one man's disobedience many were made sinners, so also by one Man's obedience many will be made righteous."

This is a great Exchange!

Christ took our sins so we can have His righteousness.

He didn't take 80 percent of our sin, so we can have 80 percent of His righteousness! He took 100 percent of our sins, so we can boldly say we have 100 percent of His Righteousness!

Hallelujah!

Isn't *that* **Good News**?

Romans 3:24, "Being justified freely by his grace through the redemption that is in Christ Jesus"

Not by your work (Ephesians 2:9), but by your complete belief and trust in Him!

Prayer Of Salvation

Glory to God!

Confession

Heavenly Father, I thank you, for I am righteous! Not by work but by Grace, by what your son Jesus Christ has done for me on the cross of Calvary, I am in right standing with God.

Everything that was ungodly and sinful about me was taken away from me by the death and the Resurrection of Jesus!

Now I can boldly say: I am the righteousness of God in Jesus Name!

Amen.

Testimonials and Contacts

Hallelujah!

If you are not yet born again, please read this prayer to receive Jesus Christ as your Lord and Personal Saviour:

"Dear heavenly Father, I believe in Jesus Christ the Son of the living God.

I believe He died for me and God raised Him from the dead.

I confess with my mouth that Jesus Christ is the Lord of my life from this day forward.

I give my life to Jesus Christ and I open my heart by faith to receive salvation in Jesus name,

Amen."

If this book has been a blessing to you, or if you have been saved by reading this book, we would like to hear your story.

Please contact us at the following address.

Contact information

Higher Life in Christ Int'l Ministries
Fürstenbergsgatan 4
416 64 Göteborg
Sweden

Internet

E-mail: pastordavid@higherlifem.org
Web page: http://www.higherlifem.org

Donations

If you would like to support our work in spreading the Gospel of God's Grace, we would greatly appreciate a donation through one of the following means.

Bankgiro: 733-1382
SWISH: 123 245 47 00

Give through International Bank Transfer:
IBAN number: SE8880000810599642555297
BIC: SWEDSESS

"Give, and it shall be given unto you; good measure, pressed down, and shaken together, and running over, shall men give into your bosom." (Luke 6:38)

CHRIST MISSION INTERNATIONAL

Christ Mission International is a non-profit organization dedicated to the reaching the unreached and giving hope to the hopeless.

Feed a child by supporting Christ Mission. There's a lot of kids going around hungry, but with your help we can make a difference.

Swish: 123 188 41 13
Paypal: info@christm.org
Bankgiro: 113-8759
FromOutside Sweden:
IBAN:
SE80 8000 0810
5992 4843 0085
Bank BIC:
SWEDSESS
Account Name:
CHRIST MISSION INTERNATIONAL

www.ingramcontent.com/pod-product-compliance
Lightning Source LLC
Chambersburg PA
CBHW020909090426
42736CB00008B/548